DO YOU THINK I'M BEAUTIFUL?

BIBLE STUDY AND JOURNAL

Katie

Dance!

Angela

OTHER BOOKS BY ANGELA THOMAS

Prayers for the Mother to Be

Prayers for New Mothers

Tender Mercy for a Mother's Soul

Do You Think I'm Beautiful?

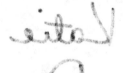

DO YOU THINK I'M BEAUTIFUL?

BIBLE STUDY & JOURNAL

A Guide to Answering the Question
Every Woman Asks

ANGELA THOMAS

Publishers Since 1798

THOMAS NELSON PUBLISHERS®
Nashville

A Division of Thomas Nelson, Inc.
www.ThomasNelson.com

Published in Nashville, Tennessee, by Thomas Nelson, Inc.

Unless otherwise noted, scripture quotations are from the HOLY BIBLE: NEW INTERNATIONAL VERSION®. Copyright © 1973, 1978, 1984 by International Bible Society. Used by permission of Zondervan Publishing House. All rights reserved.

Scripture quotations noted NKJV are from the New King James Version. Copyright © 1979, 1980, 1982 by Thomas Nelson, Inc, Publishers.

Scripture quotations noted THE MESSAGE are from *The Message* by Eugene H. Peterson. Copyright © 1993, 1994, 1995, 1996, 2000. Used by permission of NavPress Publishing Group. All rights reserved.

Scripture quotations noted CEV are from THE CONTEMPORARY ENGLISH VERSION. © 1991 by the American Bible Society. Used by permission.

Scripture quotations noted KJV are from the KING JAMES VERSION.

ISBN 0-7852-6223-7

Printed in the United States of America

06 07 08 VG 8 7

For

Sue Dee,
Karen Ellison,
Carla Martin,
and
Andrea Morgan

Thank you for teaching me so much more
about our beautiful dance in the Father's arms.

CONTENTS

INTRODUCTION

I guess I've wanted to dance as long as I can remember. Actually, I took ballet in the first grade, but then my teacher moved away. Things must have been busy back then, and somehow there were never any more lessons. I think my parents would have given them to me if I had asked. But I just didn't know how to ask, and they didn't know that I wanted to dance. In college, I enrolled in beginning ballet as a P.E. elective. I bet you can imagine a room full of coeds in leotards and tights, poised at the bar in third position, begging their bodies to cooperate with the instructor. We were all a little too late in life. Prima donna—ness had passed us by. It was fairly pitiful. I won't even describe that tippy-toe-run-and-leap thing we tried to do. Embarrassing.

I should probably tell you that I have always envisioned myself singing while I am dancing. A total "Broadway babe" wanna-be. My children bear the burden of my secret longings. Many nights, dinner comes to them via some goofy off-key song with butchered lyrics, complete with tap dancing, twirls, and *ta-da* effects at the end. They remain unmoved. It's just Mom again. Familiarity has bred boredom. They all thought I was really funny when they were nine months old.

But still I love to dance, and lack of training doesn't keep me down. It's just that I don't spend much time at the places where people are groovin'. Because I was raised at the bottom of the Blue Ridge Mountains and now live at the foot of the Smoky Mountains, I love all kinds of mountain dancing and music. My best friend was shocked to learn that I can clog like nobody's business. (In case I just lost you, clogging is a kind of down-home Riverdance.) Actually, I'll dance to anything—country-western, Carolina beach, bluegrass, funk, Sweet Baby James Taylor, or Frank Sinatra. It all makes me very happy.

I guess that's why the notion of dancing in the arms of God speaks to me. Dancing is for celebration and dancing is for fun and dancing is for romance. I love the idea of sharing all that with the God of heaven . . . the Lord of the Dance, if you will.

I have met some people who struggle with the idea of dancing and God in the same sentence. Here's my take on it: As soon as my babies could grab hold of something and pull themselves up, they would bop and sway to the beat of *boom-chick-a-boom* or Barney screaming or Bocelli singing. Their great delight over anything made their feet move and their eyes twinkle and their arms wave. It seems to me that they came prewired to wiggle and giggle over joy. And it seems as though the Creator wanted the created to dance as a celebration of delight. Don't you remember David in the Bible, who was so overwhelmed by God's love that he danced in His presence?

So I'm okay with illustrating our relationship to God through the pictures and thoughts of our dancing in His arms. I hope it speaks to some of the longings deep inside of you as well.

WHERE WE'RE GOING

I hope this isn't just another "workbook" for you. Actually, I hate it when a workbook becomes busywork and nothing powerful happens. What a waste of time and effort. I am praying that somehow these pages will become your next steps toward a deeper relationship with God. I am asking God to bring power and change into your life through these weeks of study and reflection. I hope that some layers begin to fall away so that you can start to see the woman God created and loves. The woman who may have been lost or forgotten in the blur of your life.

You will read my stories in *Do You Think I'm Beautiful?*, but these next pages are all about you and the God of heaven. How do you hear from Him? How will you respond? Your heart's desires. The places you stumble. The things you've never said, or the thoughts you've begged everyone to hear. These pages are about your journey and God's leading at this bend in the road. These words and questions and thoughts are about becoming something different from what we have been and opening ourselves up to dream and live with abandon.

May you sense the astounding presence of God. May you know the exhilarating freedom that comes from truth. May we all be changed from this likeness into His, from our weakness unto His strength, moving from the bondage of fear onto the victory of courage.

THE TROUBLE WITH BIBLE STUDIES AND JOURNALS

The trouble with introspection and self-description is that it makes me squirm. I never really understood why until recently. The reason I squirm on the inside when some workbook asks me to describe myself is because I haven't known who I am. I haven't known the heart of the woman inside of me. For some reason, I have been afraid to look. Afraid I'd be even more disappointed. Afraid there wasn't anything noble or interesting to be discovered. This Bible study and journal might make you squirm. You could find yourself uncomfortable or frustrated in these pages. I kind of hope you do. But I hope even more that you push past the uncomfortableness and find out what you're afraid of.

If you feel angry over a question, then go slow. If you can't answer, ask why you can't answer now and come back later. Expect to be stirred at some point, so leave yourself pliable to God's moving in your soul. If God stirs you emotionally, then engage emotionally with what He's doing. If you feel frustrated, then find out why.

There is another problem with this kind of study. Getting honest with yourself is painful and scary enough sometimes, but what if someone else reads your stuff? A woman asked me when I told her we were writing this guide, "How are you going to get women to tell the truth? I'm afraid if I write the truth then someone is going to look over my shoulder, or worse yet, my husband will read what I've written." She made a good point. If you have to be guarded, there is little hope that significant change will happen.

I'd love for you to be doing this study in a small group of women. Maybe you can make a commitment right off the bat that all writing is private unless someone chooses to share. Then you could ask your family for the same courtesy. I want you to be free to write, even if God is the only one you share your heart with.

We've left lots of space to journal, write your prayers, God's answers, diagrams, silly pictures, or anything that can reflect your thoughts and emotions during this journey. Let the journaling be a monument of sorts. Write down what God says and does through this message so you can go back and remember His answers and His leading.

One more thing—my friend said that I should warn you not to expect the man in your life to get it. She told us about reading *Beautiful* and wanting to have a rousing conversation with her husband because she was excited about the material. He is a thinking man and very interested in most things. But she said he didn't get it and he didn't really want to get it. She felt deflated, and yet her girlfriends totally related to her enthusiasm. Essentially, this book is a girl thing, and most guys, God bless 'em, aren't so into it. It's okay. We're talking about the feminine soul, and I have not to this day figured out the masculine one. So just lay down the expectations. Enjoy the journey with some girls. Save the man you love the agony of trying to figure out what you're talking about.

ALL THIS IN PRAYER

I want to ask you to commit to more prayer than you may be accustomed to. My words may be a little vessel of sorts, but the real-life change will happen because you have been in the presence of God in prayer. Prayer is where a weak woman becomes strong, and there is where she is transformed into an overcomer, a strong believer, a woman who is courageous and alive.

Many times I will ask you to write out a prayer. Go ahead and give it a shot. Sometimes you might need to ask someone else to pray for you about an emotion you feel or a lie you keep believing. Push past comfort in those times and ask for prayer.

But mostly, just pray your way through this material. I want you to hear God more than I want you to hear anything. Learn to know His voice.

Okay, enough introduction. I hope this is one of the most fun things you've ever done. I'm praying for God to astound you with His presence and His grace. I hope you learn to dance the dance of your life in the Father's arms.

— Angela

June 2003

DO YOU THINK I'M BEAUTIFUL?

If there is a question attached to the soul of a woman,
maybe it's "Do you think I'm beautiful?"

What a journey we are getting ready to take together. I am so excited to run alongside you for these next chapters. Please know that I am praying like crazy for God to speak to your heart in amazing, God-sized ways. I am expecting more of what He has already been doing, telling women that they are beautiful and watching what happens when they begin to live as if it's true.

I am asking that you reread chapter one in the book before we begin. That way, the stories will be fresh to you and we'll be on the same page in regard to thoughts, questions, and ideas.

Be prepared . . . we're going backwards in this chapter. Remembering can be delightful, but then sometimes, remembering can be painful. Would you pray right now and ask God to give your memories clarity and purpose? And while you are praying, would you also ask for the courage to be truthful? Sometimes the most powerful insights come because we have finally let the truth out of its hiding place.

Do you have some junior-high or high-school pictures of yourself lying around, or maybe some yearbooks stuffed into a box in the attic? This would be a great time to pull them out. It is amazing how the power of a picture can help us remember.

8th Grade   *9th Grade*

YOUR STORY

Before we even knew what hit us, we were had. Our minds and esteem have been shaped and manipulated by junior-high words and high-school heartbreak. We never saw it coming or had any idea that it would matter for a lifetime. What they thought of us or never thought of us did its work in our heads, and now we're trying to undo the damage and find the beautiful woman who got lost in the scuffle.

You've read the story of my growing-up days. You've heard how those years shaped my thoughts about beauty. I had always been the girl no one noticed. An afterthought when compliments were handed out. The girl no one wanted to "go steady" with. The brainy nerd who tried too hard to please. Now it's your turn to relive those foundational years. What is your growing-up story? I'll try to help you remember with these questions:

Describe your elementary years. Do you remember being a leader or a follower? What were your favorite childhood games? What did you do in the summers? Describe a couple of your closest friends back then.

I was such a follower. Most of my significant childhood was spent doing whatever my cousins wanted to do. I was very happy to make them happy. I don't remember ever being assertive enough to have my own ideas.

Let's move on to junior high and high school. Ultimately, did you feel noticed socially? If so, what memories do you have of being seen and enjoyed by your family, a friend, or a teacher?

Angela, I am really struggling with remembering my story. From my earliest memories I have been called beautiful. I remember at the age of four being told that I was pretty just before I was molested. In the next years, they always said the same things just before they grabbed me and raped me. I never wanted to be beautiful anymore.

— Erin

Did anyone notice your strengths or passions and affirm the gifts they saw in you? Who was it? What did they say? How did it make you feel?

_____

_____

Were there boyfriends or just the names of boys you wrote on your notebooks? Who were they? Do you remember what made those guys attractive to you?

_____

_____

I told you that the summer before my senior year in high school, I discovered contact lenses, got my braces off, and tried a Farrah Fawcett haircut—all within a week or so. I was completely changed on the outside. Maybe even pretty if you tilted your head and squinted. But the die had already been cast on the inside. I knew that I would never be beautiful.

By the end of high school, what die had been cast in your heart and your soul with regard to beauty?

_____

_____

Take a minute to write out a list of ten adjectives that describe you from the inside out.

_____

_____

_____

Did you include the word _beautiful_ in your description? Why or why not?

_____

_____

Many in our parents' generation were very pragmatic. So while things of beauty were wonderful, they were not so highly valued or pursued. There wasn't any time for all the fuss and bother. Eyes down. Work hard. Play little.

Were you affected by a lack of beauty or appreciation of beauty in your growing years?

_____

_____

_____

GROOVIN' FROM THE EDGE

Okay, you know the whole Cinderella story front to back. You love the part where the glass slipper fits, just like I do. Now let yourself become one of the characters. Which one do you allow yourself to become and why?

Most of us learned the hard way . . . Cinderella is always someone else. Somewhere along the way, we decided to come to terms with the fact that we were muddling through our lives unseen, unknown, and unheard. We learned to stand around the edge of the room in our best ball gown and just groove. Smiling and pretending.

But some of you have had "Cinderella moments" when you felt noticed and called out. Was it prom night or your wedding or some other special occasion? Try and remember as many "Cinderella moments" as you can.

Maybe there were a few Cinderella moments for you, but it never quite all worked out. Maybe you danced, but no one ever came looking for you later. Maybe the glass slipper fit, but the *happily ever* didn't come *after*. Maybe

> ### A LITTLE BIBBITY-BOBBITY-BOO
>
> *I have a friend who immediately said that she had always thought of herself as the fairy godmother. I find it interesting that I hadn't even considered her as one of the options. My friend believed that the more fun role would be granting everyone's heart's desire. I had always thought that the whole point was being the girl who was asked to dance. What an interesting insight into my friend. Why can't I ever think outside the box like that?*

you learned to pretend that it didn't matter. But do you remember that you were made feminine, wired with the desire to be seen and known and loved deeply? It's okay to want what you were made for. It's okay for you to desire to be known as beautiful. It's okay to want to be Cinderella.

Are you feeling some hesitancy when I tell you these longings are okay and encouraged in your feminine soul? What makes you hesitate?

_____

_____

Has it been easier to pretend that the whole beauty thing doesn't matter to you, or to only give a nodding glance to its importance?

_____

_____

How would your family react if they knew that you longed to be known as beautiful?

_____

_____

How has your church or heritage influenced your thinking or pretending?

_____

_____

Have you become a sensible woman with all kinds of insulation techniques? What have you been doing to protect yourself and hide from your true heart? What lies have you concocted to make life hurt less?

_____

_____

_____

Maybe as a child you weren't allowed to pursue beauty or beautiful things. What is God saying to you now?

_____

_____

_____

NO MORE PRETENDING

Some women live an entire lifetime, die, and go to heaven, pretending and smiling politely. I can barely stand the thought of it. In some very profound ways, I am thankful that one day it finally all came undone for me. Every prop was knocked down. Every place to hide revealed. For the first time, my soul was ripped open, and the truth came pouring out. Alone and empty, my heart begged to know, "Oh God, do You think I'm beautiful?"

Now it's your turn. Dog-ear this page in the book because you're going to come back here. Would you write out a prayer? Ask God if He thinks you're beautiful. And then boldly request an answer. I want you to date this one when you're done. Ask God to be loud and lavish when He answers. Ask Him to speak to you in ways that are unmistakable and in your own love language . . . in ways that you would under-stand and that would help you realize it's Him.

Your job is to pray and then look and listen for God's answer. When He answers—and He will—come back here and record what He says.

Do you understand that the question, "Do you think I'm beautiful?" is really yours to ask? Truly. God wants you to ask and then hear what He has to say about you. So pray. Wait. Listen.

Let's stop here for a moment and look at the idea of truth from Scripture. When

My Prayer   *Date:*

_____

_____

_____

_____

God's Answer   *Date:*

_____

_____

pretending stops, then we are left with truth. Look up these next passages in your Bible. Think and write about how each one of these ideas about truth could apply to your journey right now. How is God asking you to pursue truth in regard to the question, "Do you think I'm beautiful?"

John 8:32

_____

_____

Psalm 51:6

_____

_____

Philippians 4:8

_____

_____

When pretending ends and truth begins . . . it can actually turn out to be kind of scary. Pretending women have become pleasers just to find some sense of acceptance. When the props fall away, then we're left with ourselves. I realized that I did not have any idea who I was or what my true heart desired. I didn't know if I liked blueberries better than strawberries or vice versa. I liked whatever was going to please most of the people in the room. I still don't have all the answers, but I am learning to embrace the truth of my likes and longings.

It's time to do a little heart work. Who are you really? What do you like, and what do you long for? These questions are tough, so you may have to come back to this section several times after some thought and prayer. Ask God to amaze you with the beauty of your true heart.

Many of us have become shut down to the things we might have wanted or what we dreamed of doing with our lives. You could possibly remain shut down and numb

for the rest of your days. I believe this is more than just a workbook and some busy-work to pass your time. There is a purpose for this study at this point in your life. Is God calling your soul awake? Could He be shouting the truth of His devotion to you, but this time you're going to hear Him?

So stop fidgeting. Don't skip over this. Don't look on someone else's paper. Just rest. Linger. This is about you. Just you. Doggone it, what do you like? What would you choose to do with your life if it didn't matter what anyone else said or thought? Try to answer these prompting questions from your true heart.

If you could decorate any room in your house the way you wanted to, which room would it be? How would you decorate it? (Assume that money is no object.)

_____

_____

_____

_____

Plan a perfect evening for yourself from dusk to sunrise. Extravagant dreaming encouraged.

_____

_____

_____

_____

_____

_____

If you went back to school, what is the first course you'd take?

_____

_____

_____

_____

_____

If it weren't too late to learn a new sport or activity, which one would it be?

_____

_____

Have you ever been pampered? Can you receive the gift with gratefulness or do you worry that you don't deserve such extravagance?

_____

_____

When do you think you shine? Cut the humility and be honest. What is your absolute best thing?

_____

_____

_____

Name two things that you want to change about your life that require more courage than you have.

_____

_____

_____

Do you feel you can make up your mind on your own, or have you always looked to someone else to validate your thoughts?

_____

_____

SARAH TELLS THE STORY OF GOD'S PAMPERING:

There was a woman who worked in a rather expensive beauty salon. It wasn't the kind of place I'd ever be able to afford. I had known her for several years, but only as a passing acquaintance. One day she called me and said, "I'd like to give you a gift. I'd like to give you a facial every month, and color and cut your hair for free when it's needed." I almost didn't say yes because I was so surprised by her generosity. I couldn't understand why she'd want to do that for me. She said that something inside of her felt compelled to call and give her time and talent. It's been a year and a half since that call, and I am still receiving her "beautiful gifts" every month. I finally realized that God was the giver of this blessing and that He was pampering one of His beloved.

Do the important people in your life think your ideas are important, or do they mock your opinions?

THE POWER OF THE QUESTION

If there is one thing I want you to get from this chapter, it is permission to ask, "Do you think I'm beautiful?" Good grief, I know how hard this is. We aren't supposed to ask this stuff out loud. Believe me, I'll be taking ribbing about the title of this book until the day I die. If one more person says, "Hey, Angela, I think you're beautiful," I think I'll croak. I know they mean well. But they were prompted, and it doesn't count when someone is prompted.

Anyway, I realize how difficult it is to cut through your busy life and all the demands you try to juggle. Now a girl in a book is asking you to try and find your real heart. It probably feels easier just to close the book and not think about it. But wait—don't do that yet. I'm afraid you might keep living the same way you've been living for another thirty years if you don't at least try.

There is a woman inside of you who was designed by God. She was made to long for passion and romance and love. She came here with a set of gifts and talents that look like none other. She was made for beauty and to long to be known as beautiful. She has gotten lost somewhere in the journey of your life, and I want you to find her. I want you to become reacquainted with the woman God thought of when He thought of you.

It may be easier for you to believe this question belongs to every other woman but you. But it is truly yours. It came attached to your soul. God wants you to ask Him because He loves to answer. Remember? The king is enthralled by your beauty (Psalm 45:11).

I imagine that God has been trying to speak into your heart for a very long time, but maybe you are just beginning to wake up to His great joy over you. Could you possibly learn to believe that God likes you and wants to pamper you? Maybe you have intellectual knowledge. You believe the Bible verse in your head. To make the transfer from your head to your heart is a work of the Holy Spirit.

Ask God that, by the power of the Holy Spirit, you would begin to believe in your heart that the king [God] is enthralled [captivated] by your [my] beauty.

God is captivated by my beauty.
Can you say that out loud?
God is captivated by my beauty.

Would you make a list of words that describe the beautiful woman you long to be?

_____

_____

_____

_____

_____

_____

Now write out a prayer asking God to wake you up, renew your mind, speak to your doubts, and give you understanding. Ask Him to do an incredible life work in these weeks. Ask Him to start something big with you. Ask Him to make you the woman you just described above.

_____

_____

_____

_____

I sought the LORD, and He heard me,
And delivered me from all my fears.
They looked to Him and were radiant,
And their faces were not ashamed. (Psalm 34:4–5 NKJV)

When I finally know something to be true in my heart,

it's like making eye contact with God.

Chapter Two

THE WALLFLOWER
WHO IS ASKED TO DANCE

If there is a question attached to the soul of a woman, maybe it's "Do you think I'm beautiful?" When God answers from the depth of His great love, it makes some of us feel like the wallflower who is asked to dance.

Yesterday my kids had the day off from school for a teacher's convention. Evidently the local skating rink wanted to take advantage of a schoolful of kids with nothing to do, so they opened for a special afternoon session with a discounted rate. My third grader, Grayson, came home with all the details written in his agenda. Two of my other children who attend the same school hadn't heard a thing about it, but we decided to get ourselves over to the rink the next day to see if anything fun was going on.

Sure enough, when we got to the skating rink, there was a sign on the door welcoming the kids and parents from our school. Grayson was right, as usual. I paid nineteen dollars for all of us to skate and some of us to have roller blades. We just happened to be the first ones there, so we quickly traded in our shoes and hurried out to the huge wooden floor. A little time passed, but no one else showed up. Just the two guys who worked there and us. At first the kids were whining about wanting other kids to come, but then eventually they realized it was pretty cool to have an entire skating rink to ourselves, complete with concession stand and yell-to-the-DJ special requests.

The manager was obviously losing money. I don't think you can rent a skating rink for nineteen dollars these days, but he was so great to our family. He cranked up the fog machine, played all the crazy games with just us (how long has it been since you danced through a limbo line on skates?), worked the multicolored lights and the mirrored ball, and played our favorite songs, even indulging this mom's penchant for Motown.

Anna Grace skated with her hands in my back pockets for most of the day. We did Y-M-C-A, the Hokey Pokey, and a skater's form of Simon Says called "Red Light, Green Light" where I showed two little boys that their mom can still take them on any day. The children wanted Sprite and big, fat dill pickles for a snack. Yuck. And I guess we danced and raced around that rink for a solid two hours without another soul in sight.

The kids ended up with blisters and my legs were rubber, but, wow, did we have a blast. It was so fun giggling, falling, and dancing together. We just about forgot that anything was wrong with the world, and for a while there, my four kids were holding hands, skating in a line together, forgetting that they were siblings who always point out what's wrong with each other. It was just the best gift right in the middle of our crazy week. We all left with big smiles plastered to our faces.

Many years have passed since I was the high-school wallflower who was asked to dance, but yesterday reminded me what it felt like. I was dancing on wheels with the people I love most in the world. We were singing as loud as we could to our favorite music. No one was standing in the shadows afraid to try. Each of us was completely given over to joy, the pure pleasure of celebration, the great delight of dancing just because you're alive.

I imagine that God smiled as He watched us enjoying His gift . . . a private skating party for five, all for the low, low price of nineteen dollars. God, thank You again for the stuff we don't deserve, surprises that renew our hearts and the blessing of dancing with the ones we love.

This chapter is about being seen across the room of heaven and earth, called by name and asked to dance the dance of your life in the arms of God. And then, it's about what happens when a woman gets that close to God, the place where she is safe and vulnerable and free to ask anything else that her soul longs to know.

If you haven't read this chapter in a week or so, go back and reread it before you dive in.

Pray and keep asking others to pray for you. Remember, these weeks are important.

We aren't just talking about recipes or how to decoupage coffee cans. This is about coming to see yourself through the eyes of God. It could change your whole life. Be faithful to cover this time in prayer.

THE WALLFLOWER

Do you have a wallflower story? Write about your story here.

_____

_____

_____

How about the first time you were asked to dance or your first date? Write down the details you remember.

_____

_____

_____

_____

What emotions seem to rise to the surface as you remember?

_____

_____

I was a wallflower, but some of you weren't. Our stories will each be different, but the truth about God is the same. He sees you, and He sees me. You have captured His attention, and He invites you to dance in His arms.

Dancing, for me, means living in the fullness of my gifts and passions. Drinking deeply of relationships, adventure, and learning. Dancing means being fully alive and in step with the movement and plans of my Father. I don't want to miss anything God had in mind for me. I want to grow and become and change. I call it dancing in His arms.

As you know by my story, sometimes I have wondered if the wallflower role was my calling in life . . . always watching and never truly entering in. I felt my feet want to, but I'd say to myself, "Nah, quit dreaming about dancing and go make dinner."

How would you fill in this blank?

Quit dreaming about _____ and go make dinner.

    I am hoping you just wrote the truth of your longing, that thing inside of you that sets off the passion siren. Have you heard the shrieks of your passion lately? Or have they been silenced by the weight of your life? The spin of your family? The time already passed?

    Did you know that the God of heaven is speaking your name? Calling your passions alive? Inviting you into the romance of His love? I imagine that as you are reading this book God is beginning to stir something inside of you.

> *He shuffles to my locker. Skinny Steve with the zits. Yuck! Probably wants to ask me to the dance.*
> *My last chance. Oh, well. Better than being a wallflower, like Jenny.*
> *Deep Breath. "Hi, Steve."*
> *"Hi, Sue."*
> *"You wanted to ask me something?"*
> *Even his zits blushed.*
> *"I wondered . . . do you have Jenny's phone number?"*[1]

Journal about those stirrings. How are you hearing God call your name? What is going on with your passions and giftings? How is God calling your soul awake?

    One author says that there are seven longings of the human heart that do not need to be repented of. He believes that we came with these longings on purpose, and they will either be met in God and in relationships He provides, or we'll find a way to meet those longings outside His provision in sin.

    What do you think of these longings, listed below? Do you see these desires behind the way you live your own life, or have you tried to deny their existence or importance? Journal your thoughts about each one.

This is the most difficult part of this book for me. I am at least 150 pounds overweight. Because of stress and poor habits, I seemed to put on more and more weight as time went by. My husband of 23 years just left me and our three children. There is no "other woman" that he is running to. He is just running away from me and our miserable marriage. Now you are telling me that God wants me to dance in His arms. Nobody wants me. I am struggling with the idea that God could really want me.

—Julie

1. The longing for assurance that we are loved.

_____

_____

2. The longing for enjoyment.

_____

_____

3. The longing to be beautiful.

_____

_____

4. The longing to be great.

_____

_____

5. The longing for intimacy without shame.

_____

_____

6. The longing to be wholehearted and passionate.

_____

_____

_____

7. The longing to make a deep and lasting impact.[2]

_____

_____

At first read, you may consider your longings and find that simply numbness—or nothing—will come to mind. That is normal for a woman who has shut down her heart in the effort to make life hurt less. As these weeks go by, keep pursuing God on this one. Come back to this page and these thoughts. He will take you deeper as you press into Him.

Do you need to ask God to give you permission to desire again? Go ahead. Ask Him. He wants you to desire a significant life. He wired you to long for beauty. Is there a passion that stands in the shadows of your life? Something inside of you that longs to dance again or for the very first time? A yearning that was built into your design, placed there by God? Ask Him to show you specifically what you long for and where you have been hindered or how your heart has shut down. Ask Him to release you into a passionate life.

Some of you know what you are passionate about. What needs to happen in order for you to give yourself permission to dream about your longings again? Do you need the man you love to give you wings? Do you need someone else to believe in you? Remember those people you asked to pray for you? Would you ask them to pray about this with you and for you?

INTO YOUR EYES

Find Psalm 45:10–11 in your Bible. Write out those verses here, substituting your name wherever possible:

_____

_____

_____

_____

_____

Remember that *enthralled* means "captivated, smitten, fascinated, spellbound, and delighted." Have you ever considered that *enthralled* is how God feels about you? How does your heart respond to hearing that God is enthralled with your beauty? Do you hesitate when you hear these ideas? What holds you back?

_____

_____

_____

_____

_____

_____

Romance. Passion. Dancing. **These aren't the words we usually use to describe our relationship with God. But do they ring true with your soul? When you are brutally honest with yourself, isn't passion what your heart longs for? Why or why not?**

Maybe the thoughts of romance were ruined for you years ago. An awful relationship or marriage. Terrible childhood memories of molestation or worse. Did you know that God never intended romance to be ugly? His creation of this kind of intimacy is pure and without pain. If you need to, would you ask Him, right here, to begin changing the ideas you associate with romance. Write out a prayer that gives God your hesitancy and fears.

I believe that romance and passion are incredibly beautiful gifts that the Father gave us. And the longing to be known intimately is a desire that came attached to the soul. We don't have to be ashamed for longing to be held and loved. It's okay to want what you were made for.

THE GOD THING

Why does it have to be the God thing? Remember that whole interaction with my hair guy? It still makes me smile, but the truth of the question is incredibly real to most of us. Either we still wrestle with our understanding of God or someone around us questions why it has to be about Him.

You know that very little in this workbook is going to make sense if you haven't nailed down what you believe about the reality of God. There are so many dimensions to this amazing God of ours, but I want us to review a few of His names and attributes here before we go any further.

God, the Creator

This is where the whole idea of you came from. God dreamed you before you ever were. He fashioned you in the image of one He adores.

> For you created my inmost being;
>> you knit me together in my mother's womb.
> I praise you because I am fearfully and wonderfully made;
>> your works are wonderful, I know that full well.
> My frame was not hidden from you
>> when I was made in the secret place.
> When I was woven together in the depths of the earth,
>> your eyes saw my unformed body.
> All the days ordained for me
>> were written in your book
>> before one of them came to be. (Psalm 139:13–16)

Journal your praise or thoughts about God as our Creator.

God, the Father

In the Gospels, Jesus uses the word *Abba* to refer to God. Literally translated, *Abba* means "daddy." In our great and awesome God, there abides the heart of a Father . . . Daddy. And we can come to Him believing that He cares for us and interacts with us with all the compassion and tenderness of a daddy who fusses over his beautiful daughter. Maybe your earthly dad never acted like he was smitten or taken with you. Do not let his selfishness tarnish the truth of your Daddy in heaven . . . our God who longs to hold you in the arms of His strength and provision.

Jesus said that:

His miracles came from the Father (John 10:32).

He only does what the Father instructs him to do (John 8:28).

No one can snatch you out of the Father's hand (John 10:29).

More of the New Testament says that:

The Father gives grace and peace (Ephesians 1:2).

Every good and perfect gift comes to us from the Father (James 1:17).

And the writer of Psalms said that:

God is a father to the fatherless (Psalm 68:5).

Do you have anything you'd like to say to your Father? Do you need to hear His tender voice of direction and sense that He loves you like a daddy? Linger with your thoughts about our God who loves you with the heart of a Father. What is He saying to you?

God, the Son, our Savior

God came as Jesus Christ, the Son, to be our Savior. Knowing that His created ones would never be able to save themselves from the consequences of sin, God, in His mercy, came as Jesus to live, teach, train, and then die as punishment for the sins of the world. You and I are separated from the holiness of God by our sin. The death and resurrection of Jesus made a way for you and me to cross over into fellowship with our Almighty God. God says that when we believe Jesus Christ is His Son and that His death can cover our sins, then we can be saved from punishment.

I had known about Jesus all of my life. When I finally came to understand that Jesus died on the cross to pay for my sin, I prayed to God and asked Him to be my Savior. But then I wasn't certain, so I did the whole thing again. Then I wondered if I prayed just the right words, so I prayed again with different words. I bet I asked God to save me at least 150 times over several years. I just could not find an assurance that I had done everything perfectly.

A time finally came when I was again in front of God, asking Him to save me. I

said, "God, if there is something else I need to do to be saved, don't hide it from me. I want You. I want Your forgiveness. I want to spend eternity with You. Show me if I've missed something." I seemed to hear in my head, "Enough already. I have not hidden myself from you. You are saved forever." It's been completely settled in my heart ever since.

Most of us came to understand God as the Son and our Savior at some particular point in our lives.

What is your story? When did you first understand Jesus as the Savior?

_____

_____

_____

_____

_____

_____

God, the Holy Spirit

The Holy Spirit is the part of God that comes to live in our souls when we ask God the Son to save us. The Holy Spirit is the presence of God who gives us guidance and discernment. He reveals the sin in our lives. And He intercedes for us before the throne of God.

If we keep to the dance analogy, we might say that the Holy Spirit is the person who invites us into the arms of God. He is the voice we sense calling us into this very intimate and personal relationship.

In the book of John, Jesus promised that He would send the Holy Spirit to help us:

Maybe you haven't ever nailed down your belief about Jesus as the Son of God, our Savior. If you haven't ever prayed and asked Jesus to forgive you of your sins and be your Savior, you can right now. Use your own words and talk to God about your desire. You'll want to remember the day you turned your whole life over to God, so journal your prayer and date it. Then make sure you tell someone else who loves God about your prayer. They will want to rejoice with you and walk with you as you begin to learn more about God, our Savior.

And I will pray the Father, and He will give you another Helper, that He may abide with you forever—the Spirit of truth, whom the world cannot receive, because it neither sees Him nor knows Him; but you know Him, for He dwells with you and will be in you. (John 14:16–17 NKJV)

How do you know when the Holy Spirit is giving you direction? Ask some of your close friends in Christ how they know when the Holy Spirit is prompting their thoughts or actions.

GOD IS LOVE

What we have come to call love, the yearning inside each of us to be enjoyed by someone else and give that same joy in return, is the very nature of God.

Look up 1 John 4, a passage we'll return to later in this book, and read for yourself verses 7–18. Answer these brief questions:

Where does love come from?

In verse 15, what happens to the person who acknowledges that Jesus is the Son of God?

From verses 12 and 17, what does the love of God do in our lives?

Lest you begin to believe that the great love of God is for everyone else except you, find Ephesians 2:4–8. God wants you to understand that it is His incomprehensible love that allows Him to love sinful people—people like you and people like me. Love for the unlovable, the disobedient, the wayward, the scarred . . . it's called *grace*.

I love the paraphrase of this passage in *The Message*:

Immense in mercy and with an incredible love, he embraced us. He took our sin-dead lives and made us alive in Christ. He did all this on his own, with no help from us! Then he picked us up and set us down in highest heaven in company with Jesus, our Messiah.

Now God has us where he wants us, with all the time in this world and the next to shower grace and kindness upon us in Christ Jesus. Saving is all his idea, and all his work. All we do is trust him enough to let him do it. It's God's gift from start to finish! We don't play the major role. If we did, we'd probably go around bragging that we'd done the whole thing! No, we neither make nor save ourselves. God does both the making and saving.

This love is from God, His amazing, gracious, and completing love is meant for you. You and I are invited to dance in His arms just because of His mercy and grace. No previous experience required. Two left feet allowed. Free dancing lessons to everyone who would believe He is True. Come one, come all. The music has already started. Just follow His lead.

What are you learning about the "God thing"? Why is He the only avenue by which we will ever find the answers to our questions?

DO YOU NOTICE ME?

Maybe you still feel like the wallflower. Maybe you still can't imagine God walking across the room to speak your name. Maybe you can't believe that you have been seen and adored. Can you ask yourself why? Why haven't you ever recognized God walking across the room to call your name?

Has God allowed you to live many years in wallflowerdom so that in these moments He could shatter that image with powerful authority? Does He want you to realize now that being a wallflower is not the life He planned for you? What is your heart saying? Do you want to believe God has more for you?

_____

_____

_____

What, if anything, continues to hold you back? Prayerfully talk to God about it here:

_____

_____

_____

Recount a time when you felt wonderfully noticed.

_____

_____

_____

How does it feel to know that God appoints angels to guard your coming and going (Psalm 91:11), your waking and your sleeping? Remember Psalm 121? Our God does not sleep. His eyes are continually upon you. Nothing about your life goes unseen.

Sometimes my children will ask, "Mama, why are you staring at me?" It's just because I love to watch them do what they do. I love to quietly watch Anna Grace play and talk with her dolls. I enjoy watching Grayson show William how to build a Lego man. I love to watch them because they are mine. Even more, our God delights in noticing His created.

Would you ask God to let you know that you are noticed by Him? Ask Him to be unmistakable in letting you know that you are seen and noticed by the God of heaven. Ask Him very specifically and then date your prayer. Come back to this place when you have seen or heard His answer. Record and date what you have received from God. Let us not forget the great works of God in our own lives and that He truly does answer our prayers.

_____

_____

_____

_____

_____

IS ANYONE LISTENING TO ME?

Go ahead and write it out. When was the last time you felt unheard? This morning with the kids? Last night with your husband? This week at work? With a friend? A neighbor? Another family member?

_____

_____

_____

_____

_____

Now ask God to hear your prayers and answer your cries to be heard. Do you want someone safe to talk to? Then ask God for provision. Do you need counseling you cannot afford? Ask God again. Do you long for the ears of your children? Again, with boldness, come before the Lord and ask Him to make it so. What do you need? Go ahead and write it out here. He is waiting to hear.

Women ache for intimate connection. There is a desperate loneliness that settles on the heart not heard. Lonely for companionship. Lonely for expression. Lonely for affirmation.

Is anyone crying for help? GOD is listening,
ready to rescue you. (Psalm 34:17 THE MESSAGE)

WILL YOU RESCUE ME?

This may be a tough one for some of you. As you look over the events of your life, you may have heard yourself ask this question somewhere in your past. There may be pain associated with your remembering. Has there ever been a time when you needed to be rescued but felt abandoned by God?

_____

_____

_____

_____

Can you turn to God and ask Him where He was during the event you are remembering? This may feel intense for you. The answer may not come immediately, and you may want to walk through these prayers with a counselor or friend.

_____

_____

_____

When this happened and you did not feel the Lord rescue, what conclusions did you come to about yourself?

> I'm not worth saving.
> I deserved it.
> I was made to be used.
> It was punishment for previous sin.
> I caused it.

Remembering a painful past and then asking God for His answers may be incredibly difficult for you. Would you ask God to show you that He is a rescuing God? Ask Him to begin healing your past.

Maybe you need to be rescued from a season or place in your life. Maybe you need to be rescued from a relationship. Maybe you need to be rescued from your own choices and bad habits. This is a great time to come to God with the truth of your need.

DO YOU REALLY LOVE ME?

I guess if we want anything in this lifetime, it's deep, unfailing love. Some of us have tasted it and want more. Some of us have never known it and yet desire so intensely. And some of us have long ago given up on really being loved.

I told you that for me, the question "Do you really love me?" means:

Will you accept me in process? Will you embrace what is different about me and applaud my efforts to become? Can I just be human—strong and vibrant some days, weak and frail on others? Can I have a relationship with you without pretending? Can I be honest and expect honesty? Is it okay if my hair looks gross, my morning breath is not minty fresh, and my jeans are stretched around a few extra pounds? Will you love me even if I disappoint you? Will you love me through dark places? Will you love me even when I doubt your love?

Think about the people in your own life. Now what does the question "Do you really love me?" mean to you?

Have you heard God tell you that He loves you lately? How? When? Where?

Remember Proverbs 19:22:

What a man desires is unfailing love.

Did you realize that God's unfailing love is the love your soul was made for? You and I were made with an empty place that can be filled only by the unfailing love of God. What is going on in your life that keeps His love from being enough for you?

Sometimes we can lose our way and forget our design. Maybe you need to ask God to give you a craving for His love. A fresh desire for His filling. A yearning for the fullness that can come only from Him. Pray and ask God to make you hungry for Him.

Do you have other questions for God in regard to your hopes and dreams for love? Write them out in your own words as honestly as you would speak them to a friend.

GO AHEAD AND DANCE

Okay, we've been talking about dancing, wallflowers, and God. I have told you that God sees you across the room and thinks that you are incredibly beautiful. He is inviting you to dance in His arms. It's safe there, and you can whisper into His ear all the questions your heart longs to ask. This dance is the dance of your life. The one He envisioned when He dreamed of you.

You know, these are big truths that could impact the way you get up and face your life every day. What kind of woman would you be if you believed this stuff? What kind of life could you have if you were truly dancing? I think this is a pivotal place for you to stop, listen, and respond.

The God of heaven is looking at you, watching you stand around the edge of your life. And He is asking you to dance. What are you going to do?

My friend told me she prayed a prayer something like this:

Lord, I am standing up against the wall over here in the shadows, and I am scared. I don't really know people who dance. Nobody in my family dances. It seems like most of the people I know are afraid to go for it. They seem afraid to really trust You to lead. Maybe they are afraid they'll look like a fool. So, this seems wild to tell You that I want to dance with You. Are You giving me permission to move toward the things I've been trying to hide from all my life? My desire to be pretty? My longing to dream big dreams? My feet that want to dance and run through life with joy? God, if You're asking me to dance, I don't ever want to forget it. Would You please ask me to dance in such a way that I know it's You? I do love You, God, and I love knowing that You see me over here hiding. Amen.

Did you see the movie *My Big Fat Greek Wedding*? Everything was so over-the-top. The passion. The love. The dancing. The food. The hair. Every part of their lives was huge and wild with emotion . . . almost out of control. I left the theater feeling like the vanilla in-laws and wishing that I were Greek. I left feeling as if everything fun in life is outside my box. All the lines I had drawn around my life seemed to leave the passion out. Then one day my friend said to me, "What if God is Greek too?"

I can't tell you how much hope that gave me. What if God kissed you as though He's known you forever? What if He yelled with delight every time He saw you? What if God had never known a stranger, and His table was always overflowing and everyone was family? What if He were full of emotion concerning every bit of your life?

Anne's friend had spent a good twenty years in a very lonely marriage. No gifts. No special trips or surprises. No romance. Just two people muddling through life under the same roof. One day the woman finally cried out to God, "My husband has never brought me flowers. Why am I not special enough? Why does it have to be like this? God, I have always wanted to receive flowers. Why am I so unworthy?" That very day, a huge bouquet of flowers appeared at her door. There was no card. Her husband was just as surprised as she was. No one ever came forward to take credit. The woman knew for the first time what God thought of her . . . she was more than worthy . . . she was special and her cries, every one of them, had been heard.

What if lots of dancing and celebration and laughter were present whenever you were with God? That has to be how God is. I'd love to be in the middle of all that love. Even better, I'd love to give away wild and passionate love like that.

He who touches you touches the apple of His eye.

(*Zech.* 2:8 NKJV)

Chapter Three

THE OTHER LOVERS

If there is a question attached to the soul of a woman, maybe it's "Do you think I'm beautiful?" When God answers from the depth of His great love, it makes some of us feel like the wallflower who is asked to dance. But we can become distracted from His invitation because of the other lovers.

As God would have it, I sat down to work on this chapter today and realized it couldn't be a better day. Today is Valentine's Day. Today is the day when everybody wants to be loved by somebody. The desire to be desired by someone you desire. That craving for love wired into our souls. Today is all about the other lovers in our lives. A celebration of romance. Dreamy cards. Long-stemmed roses. Candlelight dinners. Chocolate hearts. Whispered passion. Lingering looks. And of course, dancing.

I ran three errands this morning, and, boy, is love in the air. They were hauling roses by the truckload into a kiosk at the mall. Mylar balloons were tied to every store fixture, each boasting a bigger and brighter way to say, "I love you." At the drugstore, person after person stood in line with me to buy cards, candy, and flowers. I had gone for mascara and razors, but all the hoopla sure got me in the mood. The lady who checked me out wore dangling pink-and-red lips earrings. She said she'd already gotten long-stemmed roses from her husband before she left for work. I told her it sounded as if he loved her. She said, "He'd better." I smiled to myself, figuring that he knew he'd better get her flowers too.

It's the big love day, or is it? It's not even lunchtime, and I've already talked to four people in my life who are mourning this day. One friend is thirty-eight and single. She said she just wanted to call in sick this morning, skip this day altogether. She said in a little while, she'll probably get a fruit basket delivered to her door. There will be a sweet card that says, *You are amazing. You are wonderful. We love you, Mom and Dad.* Somehow that fruit basket makes the absence of love all the more brilliant. Her heart aches to be desired, and the pain is so intense today.

My next girlfriend is married. It's just that her husband hasn't lived at home in a few years. They used to protect this day just for the two of them, a time of intimate and tender celebration. Now she just cries through it. She knows he'll be with someone else tonight. And her soul longs for the love that was and aches for the man who is gone.

My next friend did everything right. He's got the girl. Made reservations for dinner and dancing at the club. Bought diamond earrings, cards, and roses. Hubba hubba, what an evening he had planned for his love. But she just called and decided not to come. Something about a swim practice. He's devastated. Oh my goodness, how love hurts.

And then there is Carlye. Her son, Rob, died a year ago this day at thirty-four years old. She called me from the cemetery where she and Jerry were tending to his flowers. Rob's headstone reads, *Our funny Valentine.* Could there be a pain any greater? I don't think there is.

> *Nothing spoils the taste of peanut butter like unrequited love.*
> *—Charlie Brown*

There's no denying it, especially not today. We were made for relationship. We were made to fall in love and give love and be loved. We were made for the other lovers in our lives, and yet, with that can come great and severe pain.

As we dive into this chapter, you'll probably need to reread it if it's been a while. I'll try to tread softly here, because I realize for many of us, this hurts. Again, our honesty before God will bring truth. The truth of our real needs. The truth of our mistakes. The truth of God's gentle provision. Truth will make a way for healing. And the healing salve of God's love can begin to make you whole again.

I've told everyone else today, and so I'll tell you. I love you. Corny, I guess, but I really do love that you are diligently seeking the Father's arms. Willing to face the shadows where you have been hiding. I love that you want to dance.

Before we get into the deeper waters, let's splash around with fun memories. Remember and recount your first puppy love.

What about your first real kiss? Not the second-grade kind, but the real first one, the *ka-boom* kiss.

Does remembering make you smile? Just what is it about that memory that makes you grin?

At this place in your life, can you admit to a continued longing for romance and passion? Or have you labeled your desires as foolish and banished them to a faraway land?

THE OTHER LOVERS

If I am supposed to be dancing in the arms of God, and He is supposed to be enough, then why this intense need for others to give me love? What is the role of the other people who love me, the other lovers in my heart and life? Why do women spend their lives pining for the affections of men? Why do we hold on to the memories of what we have experienced and the fantasies of what could be? Why does it matter if they notice or if they call us beautiful? Why did we believe that a man would be the answer, and if the first one wasn't then maybe the second one or even the third one will be?

It's as if we're pulled in two different directions. We want to believe that dancing with God is enough, but there is an honest struggle. We still feel ourselves longing for people. God *is* truly enough, but our lives were never intended to be confined to solitary interaction with God and no one else. That would be an exasperating effort to deny our design. We were also made by God to crave the affection of others. We were made for relationship. Were made for the community of other human beings. It's just that somewhere along the way we hoped someone could make us whole.

It is amazing to finally understand there is an empty place inside of us reserved only for God and then to learn how to give and receive love from His filling of that place—His wholeness. We find ourselves confused and wandering when we try to fill our emptiness apart from God.

Remember the paraphrase of Ephesians 1:4–6?

Long before he laid down earth's foundations, he had us in mind, had settled on us as the focus of his love, *to be made whole* and holy by his love. Long, long ago he decided to adopt us into his family through Jesus Christ. (What pleasure he took in planning this!) He wanted us to enter into the celebration of his lavish gift-giving by the hand of his beloved Son. (THE MESSAGE, emphasis mine)

Let's run through some Theology 101 to track the logic of this thinking:

You and I were made—body, soul, and mind—by _____.
We were made for _____.
The part of you that longs to be filled with love is your _____.
The soul is empty, but can be made whole by _____.

There you go. Made by God, for God, with a soul that can be made whole only by His love.

I'm camping out here because the truths are so pivotal. We can't really go much further until we get this nailed down. You and I were designed to long for love, and yet the only love that will ever make us whole is the holy love of God. You and I were *made* to be loved by God. We are the object of His affection and the desire of His longings. We've gotten it confused, but that's okay. God lets us

From my feminine heart, I can still remember the names of the boys I had a crush on. But there is some sense of shame in my remembering, like it was wrong to secretly long to be noticed. Somewhere this idea came that I was supposed to deny the feminine part of me. It was unrighteous, and so it should be fully put away.

—Anna

get it right. He can mercifully change the entire course of your life with new understanding about truth.

Let's give this some more thought. Over the course of your life so far, what have you believed would make you whole? Who or what have you pursued in the hopes of filling your empty places?

_____

_____

_____

_____

How have those pursuits turned out? Have you attained a goal or won the heart of a man only to realize one day that it wasn't enough?

_____

_____

_____

_____

Spend some time writing out a conversation with God about your other pursuits. Sometimes I still catch myself putting a person or a goal on a pedestal, and I'll have to take it to God and say something like this:

God, I know better, and yet I've done it again. I have run after something as though it was going to fill my soul. Here I am with this thing and still empty. Please forgive me for chasing the wind. Please take me back into Your arms. Hold me close. Let me dance with You. Amen.

Did you realize that you were designed to fall to pieces apart from God's filling? You are supposed to feel frazzled and afraid without His strength. We will succumb to the power of temptation without God's overcoming Spirit inside of us. Finish this time of prayer by asking God for His continued refilling of your soul. Ask Him for the wholeness that comes from His love.

THE MAN

Healthy love. Wow. We are made for it. Want it. Can't get enough of it. But *healthy* is the operative word. Things can run askew for a hundred reasons, but they will forever remain off track and unhealthy if you have believed the man you love could or would or should make you whole.

Consider the following traits of healthy and unhealthy relationships.[1] If your significant relationships tend toward the right side of the page, you have probably found yourself in some very miserable patterns of relating. There is a good possibility that one of you is, or both of you are, expecting the other to give wholeness.

Healthy and Mature	**Unhealthy and Immature**
1. Allows for individuality because you are free to be yourself.	1. Feels all-consuming with the pressure to be someone to please the other.
2. Based on trust—words and actions are expressed consistently and honestly.	2. Based on distrust and fear—feel the need to guard yourself with the other person.
3. Open sharing of feelings. Free and spontaneous.	3. Closed emotionally. Shut down. Controlling and afraid of more criticism.
4. Feels free to ask honestly for what is needed and wanted.	4. Plays psychological head games trying to fish for hidden secrets.
5. Serving each other with passion. Focused and interested.	5. Sense that you are being appeased. Uncertainty. Ambivalence.
6. Welcomes closeness and is willing to risk being vulnerable.	6. Fears closeness and sees vulnerability as a threat.
7. Free to enjoy alone time and solitude without your partner.	7. Fears abandonment and loneliness upon routine separation.

8. Gives and receives unconditionally.	8. Gives in order to get. Afraid of being taken advantage of. Selfish.
9. Maintains other friendships and relationships without a threat.	9. Neglects other friendships and family members out of insecurity.
10. Does not attempt to change the other.	10. Attempts to change the other.

If you found your significant relationships plagued with unhealthy traits, I have a few recommendations:

- *Own it.* Label your relationship unhealthy and stop pretending that it's just going to fix itself.

- *Talk to God* about the place you're in, the person you love, and your great desire for health. Ask Him for direction and wisdom as you seek healing. Keep asking. Do not be timid with God. Pour it all out and beg Him for power to change.

- *Get help as soon as possible.* Really. Run, don't walk, to the nearest godly counselor and jump in with both feet. Commit yourself to the long journey back toward healthy love.

- *Don't try to do this alone.* Real healing doesn't happen because you shut yourself off from the rest of the world. Healing happens in the context of strong relationships. People who love you and want good things for your life. You need a couple of great friends to jump in with you, keep your confidences, and encourage your efforts.

Even when you have found a healthy relationship, do you remember that the man you love can never be enough to make you whole?

What practical things can you do or steps can you take to let the man in your life just be a man?

I am struggling right now with loneliness and fear. I am 33 and have been divorced for 2 years now and am searching for the romance from the Lord that you spoke so much about. I don't feel I've found that, and I catch myself still looking for it in a man. I've been alone for 2 years, and I have learned more in those desperate times of loneliness and depression than I could ever explain to someone. I think the hardest lesson I've learned is to sit and know that He is God! To sit and be still and patient for His timing and not try to meet my own desperate needs.

—Kristin

_____

_____

_____

Where have you had unrealistic expectations about this man?

_____

_____

_____

How can you be more responsible and mature in your love for him?

_____

_____

_____

THE OTHER MAN

Like it or not—your father has made a lasting impression on you.
Whether he was close or distant, present or absent, cold or warm, loving or abusive,
your father has left his mark on you.
And your father is still influencing your life today—
probably more than you realize. [2]

So much has come to our identity as women because of our relationship, or lack of it, with the other man in our lives—our fathers.

How do you think that you are "just like your dad"?

_____

_____

_____

Now identify the traits of your father that you want to avoid in your own life.

_____

_____

_____

Has his influence been good or bad, provided strength or weakness? In what ways?

_____

_____

Not only is our identity affected, so is our perception of who God is. In *Always Daddy's Girl*, Norman Wright said,

> Imagine a little girl of seven who has known only rejection and abuse from her father whom she loves dearly. At Sunday School she is taught that God is her heavenly Father. What is her perception of Him going to be? Based on her experience with her natural father, she will see God as an unstable, rejecting, abusing person she cannot trust.[3]

It is difficult to run into the arms of your heavenly Father and dance without a good understanding of who He is. If your perception of God has been tainted because of your earthly dad, this would be a good place for us to review the truths of who God wants to be in your life.

As you read through these characteristics of God, ask yourself, "Which of these do I need God to be right now?" Highlight those and look up the corresponding verses. Make some notes and pray.

He is the loving, concerned Father who is interested in even the most basic details of our lives (Matthew 6:25–34).

He is the Father who never gives up on us (Luke 15:3–32).

He is the God who sent His Son to die for us though we were undeserving (Romans 5:8).

He stands with us in good and bad circumstances (Hebrews 13:5).

He is the ever-active Creator of our universe (Psalm 8:1-9).

He died to heal our sickness, pain, and grief (Isaiah 53:3–6).

He has broken the power of death (Luke 24:6–7).

He gives all races and sexes equal status (Galatians 3:28).

He is available to us through prayer (John 14:13–14).

He is aware of and responds to our needs (Isaiah 65:24).

He created us for an eternal relationship with Him (John 3:16).

He values us (Luke 7:28).

He doesn't condemn us (Romans 8:1).

He values and causes our growth (1 Corinthians 3:7).

He comforts us (2 Corinthians 1:3–5).

He strengthens us through His Spirit (Ephesians 3:16).

He cleanses us from sin (Hebrews 10:17–22).

He is for us (Romans 8:31).

He is always available to us (Romans 8:38–39).

He is a God of hope (Romans 15:13).

He helps us in temptation (Hebrews 2:17–18).

He provides a way to escape temptation (1 Corinthians 10:13).

He is at work in us (Philippians 2:13).

He wants us to be free (Galatians 5:1).

He is the Lord of time and eternity (Revelation 1:8). [4]

Your dad was supposed to be a vessel of God's love. Maybe he has been that. Maybe he failed miserably. Maybe you have to unlearn everything you have known about fathers so that you can come to know the wild-about-you love of your heavenly Father. Don't let these pages pass in vain. If you have soul work to do in regard to your dad, then stop. Stay here longer. Seek the voice of God. Wait until you have heard Him speak into your heart. Walk as He leads. Act as He directs.

THE CHILDREN

I have four of these little rascals. Two girls and two boys. I'm crazy about them. I think about them and their schedules a lot. I worry about their tender hearts, and I pray for their protection. I could spend most of every day doing or thinking or praying for these four people. I love them so much. Almost every day I tell them how proud I am to be their mama. And I am. Glowing. Beaming. Goofy in love. I can see how some of us begin to think that such blessings as our children will fill up the emptiness, that maybe their lives can make us whole.

Do you need to let your kids off the hook? What hook do you have them on, and how can you best set them free?

_____

_____

_____

Do they feel the pressure to perform or love in certain ways just to please you? How have you laid on the pressure, and what steps can you take to change your ways?

_____

_____

Do they feel secure in your love, or have you tried to find your security in theirs? How can you increase their security, and how can you decrease any insecurity they might battle?

_____

_____

I know you know this by now: They may be great kids, but they cannot fill that empty place inside of you. It's just for God.

THE FRIENDS

I know a group of women, all in their midforties, who have just disbanded as close friends. A part of me asks, "What in the world went wrong? Don't we all know how to be kind and friendly at this point in our lives? Why does it have to be so high schoolish still?" But no. This group of loving women went their separate ways because ultimately one could not find the wholeness and depth she required. Time and time again their trips and get-togethers were plagued by deep disappointment and heartache. They would sit for hours in long discussion, believe they had begun fresh, and then the same issues would resurface.

Most of their pain happened because a few forgot the order. A girlfriend is only a vessel. She can give a part of the love. She can be fun and interesting. But she can't ever get it all right. She will come up short, show up late, and misunderstand. She is just a girl. She is just a friend to be treasured. She cannot make you whole.

Who in your life would be blessed by a card or a note declaring your friendship? Who in your life needs to know that you get a part of God's love from her place in your life?

_____

_____

_____

Is there a woman in your life who has felt undue pressure to make you whole? Is an apology in order? Does restoration need to happen?

_____

_____

_____

Some of the best relationships in my life are those with my girlfriends, but alas, the song continues: I'd ruin everything if I expected that even one of them could make me whole.

THE STUFF

As women, most of us want to surround ourselves with our interpretation of beauty. The other day, I heard a man say that when you meet a woman who lacks a touch of beauty in her life, you have met a woman who has been traumatized. I believe that he was probably right. It's a part of our nature to want our homes to be lovely and our clothes to reflect our style. I believe that choosing to pursue beautiful in our homes or in the way we dress is perfectly wonderful. It's just that when we begin to believe that stuff can fill an emptiness, then we've crossed over into unhealthy.

Let's take a few minutes with some of Jesus' words in the Sermon on the Mount. Find Matthew 6:25–33 in your Bible and answer the following:

Jesus said to not worry. Very specifically, what things did He tell us not to worry about in this passage?

_____

_____

From verse 25, what did He say is more important than food, the body, or clothing?

_____

_____

What did Jesus say about our value to the Father?

_____

_____

According to verse 27, can worrying add anything to our lives?

_____

_____

Does the Father know your needs (v. 32)? This very day, what physical needs do you have? As you are thinking and writing, pray about those needs and take each one specifically to your Father.

_____

_____

_____

_____

_____

_____

What did Jesus command of us in verse 33 (which just happens to be my life verse)?

_____

_____

_____

And what in that same verse is the promise attached to our obedience?

_____

_____

_____

How could you apply the truths of this passage to your life right now in regard to your stuff?

_____

_____

OUR DELIGHT

The attraction, need, and desire for other lovers, other intimate relationships, in our lives is a very wonderful thing. When there is spiritual and emotional health, these amazing people can touch and transform our lives in powerful ways. God uses these people to heal and restore and bring great delight into our days.

In this chapter I said that women can lust for relationship with the same intensity that men can lust for sex. How do you respond to that idea in general?

_____

_____

_____

How have you seen other women make relationships an idol or an obsession?

_____

_____

_____

Describe how women you know have set themselves up for great relationship disappointment.

_____

_____

_____

What do you think causes a woman to believe that someone or something will make her whole?

_____

_____

I have been a Christian for 26 years, and this is the first time I have truly believed that Jesus is really in love with me, finds me beautiful, and wants to be with me!! I am married to a sexual addict, and these last 8 years have left me feeling so ugly, undesirable, worthless, and alone. For the first time in my life, I realize I am being held by the one who is crazy about me.

—Stephanie

One of the very cool things about God is that the love you have tasted here on earth through the people in your life is just the beginning. He has an entire feast of love waiting for you. There is more . . . there is a filling for your heart's desire.

Before we press on into the heart of God's love for you, would you write a prayer of thankfulness? Specifically think about each person in your life that gives you a part of the love of God. Each one of those people was hand chosen by God to love you. As you list each one on your journal pages, thank God for their place in your life, and then pray for one specific need you know each one has.

_____

_____

_____

_____

_____

_____

_____

_____

_____

_____

_____

_____

_____

_____

_____

_____

Chapter Four

WHISPERS OF UNBELIEF

If there is a question attached to the soul of a woman, maybe it's "Do you think I'm beautiful?" When God answers from the depth of His great love, it makes some of us feel like the wallflower who is asked to dance. But we can become distracted from His invitation because of the other lovers and the whispers of unbelief.

I knew we would eventually get to this place, and honestly, I've been dreading it. I know I am supposed to be leading the charge here, but you must know of my own hesitancy. *Beautiful.* It's an amazing word. It's an incredible pursuit. It's still just so hard to get my head around it sometimes.

When I began working on this Bible study, my friends said, "You're going to have to deal with the body-image stuff sooner than later. You can't wait until the end of the book. Our bodies are intertwined with every part of our identity and especially the longing for beautiful." I agreed with their observations, but I still drag my heart.

I guess part of me wants to believe I am stronger than body image. That I can disconnect myself from the face in the mirror and live separately somehow. But I can't. You realize the stupidity in my wishing. It is all woven together. Our souls came inside these vessels we call bodies. The problem is that most of our lives we have looked at our bodies with our earthly eyes and then let what we have seen assign some kind of value to our soul.

Every woman I know dreams of being the most beautiful woman in the room (well, all right, most of us would settle for being one of the most beautiful women in the room), with no prompting or prodding needed. She wants to be intellectual and witty, the one with great depth and insight, peaceful and spiritual. In short, she dreams of being captivating. The heart of a woman longs for the completion and perfection we won't know until heaven. The heart just longs to go home where it belongs, with God.

Until then, body image is in your face screaming that you can't become or captivate or improve until you lose thirty-two pounds, more or less. When you get the thirty-two off, then there is a sag problem that needs the attention of a skilled surgeon. Oh yeah, those varicose veins are trouble. And that midlife acne thing too. Actually, it seems like there will always be something left to steal our peace in regard to body image. Anything and everything will be used to whisper into our ears, "Don't believe it, God couldn't really call you beautiful."

As with every other chapter in the book, you should probably reread this one before we jump in. And it won't do you any good to skip the questions that make you squirm. No one is looking. This is between you and God. Let the truth that He reveals begin to set you free. Listen in your quiet prayer time for His voice of assurance and love. Still yourself and answer freely.

I told you that one day my counselor said, "Angela, I don't think you know very much about the love of God." He caught me off guard. I'm supposed to know a lot about that kind of stuff. Instead, I had listened to the whispers of unbelief and began to speak out of

The result of my unbelief was frailty, weakness, pain, and loneliness. If you want to come undone, just begin listening to the whispers of unbelief about God.

their deceit. I had given weight to the lies in my head. I am praying that in these pages, you and I will turn away from the whispers. That we will have eyes to see and a tender heart to respond to God's love for us. I am asking God to draw us even more deeply into the strength that comes from believing. I am asking Him to shout above the whispers, so that you can hear Him call you beautiful.

Before we begin, would you ask God to make things very clear to you in this chapter? Ask Him to unmistakably highlight all the lies that whisper into your head and all the doubts that keep you from believing in the patient, pursuing, embracing love of God.

THE WHISPERS

Sometimes we hear the things we've said to ourselves. Sometimes it's the words of junior-high taunting. Sometimes it's the words we longed to hear, but no one ever said.

I think if we'll put the whispers about body image on paper, then some of their power will go away. I'll prompt you below. We're going to put your body image on paper. I know, I'm reluctant too. Just go with me here.

Start with the good stuff and do not leave this part blank. Write down five, at least five, great traits about your physical appearance. Be specific. Remember the compliments you've received in the past.

1. _____
2. _____
3. _____
4. _____
5. _____

Can you add one more?

_____

Now for the whispers. In regard to body image, go ahead and write out every frustration. Things you and I could never change, like the width of our ankles, and things you would like to make different if you could. It seems that I can recall most of the dumb things people have said to me in regard to my shape, size, color, etc. If you are beginning to remember, then write it down.

_____

_____

_____

_____

One of my friends said, "We live in a death culture. We speak death and darkness instead of speaking life and goodness into one another's lives. God is a life giver." Could it be that the whispers you have heard about your body image all these years

have caused a part of your heart to die? Have they kept you from believing the life-giving truth that God wants you to hear? If that is true and you realize that a part of your heart is dead to beauty, then journal about your thoughts here.

_____

_____

_____

_____

Do you remember that God is wild about you? Smitten. Captivated. He calls you beautiful in Psalm 45 and declares all throughout Scripture that what He says of you is true. Knowing that God purposefully created you just the way you are, what areas of your physical appearance or personality are you struggling to accept?

_____

_____

_____

_____

Are you still struggling to believe that God calls you beautiful? Ask the Lord to make it real to you in a way that lets you know that it is Him. Ask Him to help you discover your beauty. You might pray, _God please come somehow and tell me I'm beautiful. Don't use my husband, friend, mother, or father. Surprise me with the way you answer._

_____

_____

_____

_____

So many times I've told you that I want to become the woman God thought of when He thought of me. Can you try to imagine the God-version of you? I hope this doesn't sound weird, but imagine being the God who's in love with you and then tell me what He sees when He looks at you. What can you imagine He dreams for your life?

_____

_____

_____

Remembering that God has an artist's heart—He can look at a blank canvas and envision the masterpiece—ask Him to tell you what He envisions for your future. What is the rest of your story from His perspective?

_____

_____

_____

_____

_____

CLINGING TO THE WHISPERS

Very often we keep believing the same old things about ourselves and about God, simply out of habit. The messages from the media are so deeply entrenched into our culture that we have confused their voices with the voice of God. We have come to mindlessly accept what the world calls beautiful and disregard the heart and passion of our Creator. Why? Maybe it's because we don't really know much about the love of God.

> *You know the way a mother looks at her newborn. Why wouldn't the Father's heart have felt even more over me? If a mother is enthralled with her baby, then wouldn't the Father be enthralled over me, all His idea and His creation?*

I'm going to ask some pointed questions about your relationship with God. I don't mean for them to be accusations, but promptings to get us honest with ourselves. Give attention to the squirm factor. If the questions make you mad, or make you squirm, could that really be the Holy Spirit directing you toward change, greater understanding, or even repentance?

How would you rate your life with God right now?

- Close and intimate
- Surface and Sundays only
- Distant and rebellious
- Some other combination

Are you presently trusting God for anything powerful? Waiting for Him to do the impossible? If the answer is no, what in your life needs the powerful intervention of God?

Have you ever seen God work in a powerful way in your own life? How?

Tell me of a time when you sensed the embracing love of God. A time when you knew He was present and holding you close.

They say if you want to make God laugh, draw up a five-year plan for your life. How do you respond when life doesn't turn out as you'd planned? Do you run from your relationship with God, or do you lean into Him even in your disappointment and misunderstanding?

Do you live life with a sense of adventure, knowing you are held in the arms of God, or do you live hesitantly, believing one wrong move could ruin everything?

If you are a strong, capable woman, there is a chance that you struggle with pride. It is difficult to admit that you can't figure it all out and choose to believe the truths of God anyway. Is pride an issue in your life? If so, how has it affected your relationship with God?

_____

_____

Do you look more like Jesus this year than you did last year? Are you growing up spiritually? Are you becoming more and more like Him, less and less like you?

_____

_____

_____

_____

Sometimes we get stuck. Sometimes we stop growing up for a season. Life keeps us spinning for a hundred different reasons. And in the spin, our spiritual lives can fall fast asleep. Yep, you can show up at church, sit right in the presence of God, but never really get it because your soul is snoring. I don't want to beat you up. In fact, I want to lavish you with grace, but if the Holy Spirit is trying to wake up your sleepy soul, then for heaven's sake, roll over and get out of bed.

We will never become strong women of great faith without the continued pursuit of maturity. We'll talk about this more later, but for now, realize that lack of spiritual maturity will keep you clinging to the whispers.

> *Oh yes, you shaped me first inside, then out;*
> *   you formed me in my mother's womb.*
> *I thank you, High God—you're breathtaking!*
> *   Body and soul, I am marvelously made!*
> *   I worship in adoration—what a creation!*
> *You know me inside and out,*
> *   you know every bone in my body;*
> *You know exactly how I was made, bit by bit,*
> *   how I was sculpted from nothing into*
> *   something.*
> *Like an open book, you watched me grow*
> *   from conception to birth;*
> *   all the stages of my life were spread out*
> *   before you,*
> *The days of my life all prepared*
> *   before I'd even lived one day. (Psalm*
> *139:13–16 THE MESSAGE)*

LEARNING HOW TO BELIEVE

Learn how to believe that God calls you beautiful. Don't let it overwhelm you. This one is going to take time. But my, oh my, what an amazing gift it will be to your soul. Maybe one of the first steps in learning how to believe is learning what the voice of God sounds like.

In my own life, I am realizing that sometimes I have to stop and ask myself, "Am I hearing the voice of God or the voice of the accuser?" The accuser is our enemy, Satan. Anytime God begins doing a work in our lives, Satan begins a parallel work to try and distract us. When God wants to speak to us, Satan wants to interrupt so that we can't hear. He might feed us a lie or offer us an imitation to get us off track.

You realize that if you believe a lie, it affects you, even if it's not true. And so Satan will do everything he can to get you to believe the whispers. He has observed your life and knows your weak places, the buttons that get you distracted and the issues that paralyze your soul. He likes to talk about all that stuff because it keeps you from believing and living in the truths of God.

There has to be a swapping that goes on in your soul. The truth of God in exchange for the lies of Satan. You can't psych yourself into believing. This process of exchange will take time. We go forward, slide back, and then have to regain lost ground.

Let's begin here:

When I tell you that God calls you beautiful, what thoughts immediately pop into your head?

_____

_____

_____

_____

Can you discern whether or not those thoughts are the voice of God speaking truth into your life, or the voice of the accuser who wants to keep wounding you? Which one is it?

_____

_____

_____

Keep these ideas in mind as you begin to discern and look up the verses that accompany these thoughts:

- The accuser always spotlights sin, even sin that has been forgiven and covered by the grace of God. He will keep reminding you of your sin for as long as you will listen (Revelation 12:10).

- The accuser tries to bring confusion to us by planting weeds among good seed. What God has sown that is good in our lives, Satan tries to choke out with weeds (Matthew 13:38–39).

- The accuser wants to squelch the truth in our lives with lies until we are rendered completely useless and lost. He wants to drown the believer's good life and usefulness (1 Peter 5:8).

Satan	God
Spotlights sin and keeps reminding you.	Forgives sin and remembers it no more.
Tries to make you confused.	Wants to make your path clear.
Keeps you wounded with repetitive lies.	Heals wounds and replaces lies with truth.
Reminds you what the world says.	Tells you what He has said.
Disappoints us with cheap imitations.	Rewards us with real gifts and blessings.
Never stops trying another way to trip you up.	Never stops providing abundant strength for resistance.

Remember that you may need others to help you distinguish between the voice of the accuser and the voice of God. Sometimes it can feel presumptuous to embrace what God is saying as truth.

He [Satan] was a murderer from the beginning,

not holding to the truth, for there is no truth in him.

When he lies, he speaks his native language,

for he is a liar and the father of lies.

(John 8:44)

You may need people to go the journey with you. People who can help you discover what God is saying, confirm His voice, learn to discern the words of the accuser, and encourage you to stop inclining your head toward the whispers.

Is there a woman in your life to come alongside you in the journey? Who is she? Even if she is far away, pursue an honest relationship with her. My friends Dennis and Karen Larkin live thousands of miles away from me, and yet our phone calls and e-mails have been sustaining wisdom through the years in discerning the voice of God in my life.

What kind of person should you align yourself with for a spiritual journey of learning and depth?

Assuming you are a woman, you should choose another woman.

A woman of known integrity and safety. She must be the keeper of your heart.

A woman who has known brokenness and healing.

Someone who is running fast and strong toward God in spiritual things. It's great if she is a little farther down the road than you.

A woman who is alive with passion and desires adventure.

A woman who lives and gives the grace and mercy of Jesus. This one is a rare bird. Make her dinner. Clean her oven. Do anything to get next to her.

Someone who is growing and becoming, open to the work of God, even outside her theological box. Run from legalists and those who seem to have all the answers tied up with a bow.

GOD, HELP MY UNBELIEF

There are some who would have us think that we can say something positive about ourselves over and over until we believe it. That we could chant, "I am beautiful; I am beautiful," in some quiet meditation until it is so. I just say, "Gross. How stupid is that?"

There are plenty of women's gatherings that buy into the "I am a goddess" mentality. One recent movement that comes to mind is the "Sweet Potato Queens." A bunch of women who have heard the legitimate question attached to their feminine soul and decided to answer with tiaras, marching boots, glittered attire, and a raunchy "I am the Queen" attitude. I certainly understand their longing. I just disagree with their answers.

We've heard our souls long for beautiful, but believing what God says of us is the hinge upon which this whole journey turns. If you don't believe God, then how do you go on from here? Do we just default and live vicariously? Do we watch the beautiful people and track their lives of adventure? Do we relegate ourselves to observation in place of becoming?

Maybe we should map out the options here. If you choose not to believe God on this one, then what will that mean for your life? What are you choosing for yourself emotionally, mentally, and spiritually when you decide not to believe that God calls you beautiful? Or if you actually say that you believe God calls you beautiful, in what ways does that color how you live and make choices?

I so love the passage in Mark 9 where the father of the possessed son says to Jesus,

I do believe; help me overcome my unbelief! (v. 24)

There is a story of a woman teaching this passage. She said, "You've just got to believe that He's done it and it's done." Then she added, "The great danger with most of us is that, after we ask Him to do it, we do not believe that it is done, but we keep on helping Him, and getting others to help Him; and waiting to see how He is going to do it."[1] How do you come to God in regard to belief? Do you keep trying to help Him along toward the answers you want? Or have you learned to rest in your belief, trusting that whatever you ask of God, He's on it, He doesn't forget, He doesn't get distracted?

Coming to believe that God calls you beautiful means overcoming your unbelief. We can resist believing for a million reasons. Maybe you hesitate because with believing comes responsibility. If you believe God, then things might change—you would have to change your perspective and how you perceive the world and your purpose here.

What might begin to change in your life if you could rest in the truth of being known as beautiful?

_____

_____

_____

What responsibility would come to you in believing that?

_____

_____

_____

Maybe you have thought that believing means that you are finally calm and peaceful on the inside. That you are without hesitancy. Read John 11:38–44.

Jesus came to the tomb of Lazarus and asked for the stone to be rolled away. Immediately Martha said,

> But, Lord, by this time there is a bad odor, for he has been there four days.
> (v. 39)

I smile at Martha because she is so me. She is anxious and says, "But, Lord," offering her own wise observation. When you hear that God calls you beautiful, how have you been saying, "But, Lord" to him?

_____

_____

_____

Then in verse 40, Jesus said,

"Did I not tell you that *if you believed*, you would see the glory of God?" So
they took away the stone. (emphasis mine)

As you know, after the stone was removed, Jesus called Lazarus out and back
from the dead. What is so interesting to me is that Jesus was not frustrated by the
anxious "But, Lord" of Martha. Then Martha obeyed and took away the stone, even
in her anxiety, so that she could see the glory of God.

Did you know that God is not frustrated by your "But, Lords" either? Say them
to Him. Voice your anxiety. And then believe anyway. Believing anyway is the avenue
by which we get to see the glory of God.

> Then Jesus said,
> "Did I not tell you that if you believed,
> you would see the glory of God?"
> (John 11:40)

Believing does not always arise out of peace and calm. Sometimes we will be anxious or hesitant, and yet the call is to obedience. The father of the possessed son was
hesitant and weak, and yet he leaned into a trust beyond what he could imagine.
Believing is choosing obedience and responding out of trust, even when we cannot see.

**Okay, a little more application. How is God calling you to obedience with these
truths? Specifically, what steps of obedience can you take to believe that God calls
you beautiful, in spite of the anxiousness and the "But, Lords"?**

Would you write out a prayer confessing your own doubts and unbelief, understanding that God is not put off by your struggles? He does not wag a finger in disdain at your honesty.

_____

_____

_____

_____

_____

As Christian women, our pride can say, "I shouldn't need this affirmation anymore." But we were created with the need to be affirmed. I imagine that from cradle until grave, we will always long for validation, to know that someone sees our accomplishments, and as women, to know that someone calls us beautiful.

THE SHOUT

The shout is the voice of God that comes and finally drowns out all the whispers of unbelief. From the very beginning, man has been amazed that the God of the universe would come in abounding love and compassion for such as us.

> When I consider your heavens,
> the work of your fingers,
> the moon and the stars,
> which you have set in place,
> what is man that you are mindful of him,
> the son of man that you care for him? (Psalm 8:3–4)

There is a mystery in this choosing to believe. *That God is mindful of me? That's huge.* And grabbing the whole thing is a gigantic step for most of us. It's the whole enchilada to walk down these paths and begin to understand how God relates to His creation. How the God of heaven sees just you or me and knows us intimately.

Could it be that in His eyes, we can find a reflection of ourselves that we have never known before? That in His reflection we are not how we have imagined ourselves to be, nor are we thought of as we had assumed. Could it be that God has been shouting His great love all the while, but we have buried our head underneath the pillow of whispers, choosing to remain covered by the lies of this world and the deception of the accuser?

Would you cry out in prayer and in believing, "Oh God, help my unbelief!"? Ask God to come as a shout to you.

The times I have finally heard God speak into my heart are times when I have quieted myself in some way. Alone on the sofa. On my face on the floor in my closet. Outside on a hike. Some kind of quieting posture or activity to let my soul settle so I can wait and listen.

Would you commit to listening for the voice of God? Most of the time I know God is speaking when there is a thought that lines up with what I know to be true of Him and it won't leave me alone. I try to make the grocery list in my head, but it's still there. I get up and move about, but it's still there.

Ask God to speak like a shout into your soul and then come back here and journal what He says.

_____

_____

_____

_____

_____

_____

Let the truth of God's love be the exclamation that

silences the muttering in your head.

He really thinks you are beautiful.

All of you.

Inside and out.

Top to bottom.

Yep, even around back too.

Beautiful, He says.

Chapter Five

NOISE AND CLUTTER

If there is a question attached to the soul of a woman, maybe it's "Do you think I'm beautiful?" When God answers from the depth of His great love, it makes some of us feel like the wallflower who is asked to dance. But we can become distracted from His invitation because of the other lovers, whispers of unbelief, and all the noise and clutter.

The past few months I have been plagued by noise and clutter. It is so incredibly distracting. It's as if you want to dance. You hear the music in the background. But you can't enter in because the stuff in your head makes you dizzy. The noise seems louder and bigger than the invitation from God to dance in His arms.

I am realizing that I can deal with what noise and clutter I find, and then move along, only to learn a little later that new noise and clutter has come a-callin'. Is there ever a one-time-dealt-with-it-for-good cure-all? I guess not. Removing the noise and clutter from our lives is an ongoing process.

As long as we are breathing and moving about, interacting with people and family, there will be words that come to us and make us their hostages. Situations will interrupt our plans and sidetrack our travels. Days will come when we will be moving without feeling. Sometimes life seems so heavy. We can quickly begin to feel numb. And God seems far away when our heads are filled with noise and clutter.

I can work along for months, loving and living creatively, spontaneously, and deliberately. And then noise will collect in my head and clutter will trip up my heart, and suddenly I'll be stuck. I mean it, I can wake up emotionally and spiritually paralyzed, unable to sort out the overwhelming distractions that have come to me. I have learned in my years with women that you're not much different from me; we can all become distracted and stuck.

I am praying that this chapter will prompt you to acknowledge the noise in your head and the clutter in your life. And then I am asking God to make you willing to do whatever it takes to remove everything that stands between you and His embrace.

Round up a couple of strong friends. Reread the chapter in the book if it's been a while. Grab a pencil and come with an open heart. Expect God to show up. He always comes when you ask.

TURN IT DOWN IN THERE

In the last chapter we talked about the whispers of unbelief, those murmurings you hear in your head about your beauty. The murmurs that tell you not to believe God.

We all have a bunch of stuff going on in our heads, but the noise that keeps me from the dance sounds something like this:

Have I missed something? You mean this is all there is to life?

I've wasted so much time.

What was I made for?

It's all my fault.

Who have I become, and who is the real me?

My life doesn't count for much. I'm not sure it's all worth it.

My sin is too big.

My scars are too painful.

I'm an embarrassment.

I will never be beautiful.

Somebody get me out of here.

Time is running out. Hurry up and do something.

Now, this may be difficult. We don't usually take a lot of time to stop and think about these things. So begin thinking and taking inventory. What is the noise in your head? What are the questions or thoughts that seem to haunt your days? This kind of noise is almost like a thread woven through everything you do. As you become aware of the noise, come back to this place and write down your thoughts.

The noise in our head comes from a hundred places— unanswered longings, lies we've believed, fears we've embraced, choices we've made.

Sometimes we can let the noise in our heads become our false identities. We have listened to it for so long that we have come to believe the noise represents all there is of us. Sometimes women will hear labels such as *old maid, divorced, loser, slow learner, driven,* or *broken.* The labels attach themselves to our noise, and we let them define us.

What are some names that you call yourself, or that others have called you, that have become your false identity?

_____

_____

_____

Do you remember what God calls you? Write down what God says of you.

_____

_____

_____

Remember the voice of the accuser? Weed him out of this discussion. Listen for God through the Holy Spirit.

The Holy Spirit will bring conviction, but the accuser just wants to bring shame.

Ignoring the voices doesn't get you anywhere. You have to pay attention and then take those lies to God.

The Holy Spirit speaks to us about freedom and release from sin. The accuser wants to keep us in bondage.

The Holy Spirit is clear and specific about an action, attitude, or misguided beliefs. The accuser promotes confusion and blame.

The Holy Spirit prompts us toward confession and repentance so that we

can hear God's heart of love. The accuser wants us to believe that we are eter-nally condemned.

God might say, "You didn't tell the truth." The accuser would say, "You are a liar."

The Holy Spirit wants to clear out the noise that distracts you from dancing with God. The accuser wants to leave you in a heap in the shadows.

I shared with you a time of prayer I had with a counselor that took away the noise in my head. In fact, after that time of extended prayer, I remember that the silence and peacefulness inside of me seemed foreign. Almost as if I had never known such quiet and stillness before.

There may be other effective ways to deal with the voices and their accusations, but I know of only one: powerful and passionate prayer. And so, I am going to rec-ommend prayer as the tool for quieting your soul.

AN EXERCISE IN PRAYER

You may begin alone, but for this purpose, it can be helpful to ask someone to pray with you. A counselor may be helpful if you feel that the noise in your head is particularly painful. A close friend may feel safer for you. Ask God to direct.

When we tell our secrets, even if only to ourselves, they lose their power.
—Frederick Buechner

Understand, this isn't a one-time deal, but instead, hopefully, a bit of a push to get you in. Kind of like diving into the deep end of the pool instead of slowly work-ing your way down the steps. The whole idea is to learn to swim and become a strong swimmer; it's just that I'm asking you to go ahead, jump in, and get wet.

Are you afraid to pray out loud so that someone else can hear and respond to you in prayer? Try praying aloud when you are alone in the car or at home in your room. I know it feels goofy at first, but it will get you accustomed to the sound of your voice in prayer. No need to talk any differently or whisper; just speak what comes to your mind. Begin learning what it "feels" like to speak your prayers.

Refer back to your list of noises and choose one of the loudest voices. As you begin to pray through it, you may realize there is other pain or emotion attached. Take notes if you need to.

Ask God, in prayer, about the particular thought you have chosen. Ask Him where that idea came from. Who gave it to you? Where were you when you first heard it?

_____

_____

_____

Ask Him to tell you if it is true. What is He saying to you?

_____

_____

_____

Ask Him very specifically what He says of this idea in your head.

_____

_____

_____

What is His directive? What does He want you to do with it? Where does He want you to go with it? To whom would He like for you to speak, if necessary?

_____

_____

_____

Ask God for continued insight into the particular noise. Tell Him He can wake you up in the middle of the night if He needs you—whatever it takes to understand the noise and quiet the voices.

I had not been able to quiet the noise on my own, but in prayer, listening for God's truth, quiet had come like a blanket to cover me.

Remember that this kind of intense praying is not without emotion. It may be draining for you in many ways, and sometimes you have to wait until you are ready to pray, listen, and receive. On the other hand, you can't keep procrastinating or you'll never deal with the noise. That's the whole reason we're here anyway.

Your radar may go up with all this attention on yourself. You may be thinking, "I don't want to be so focused on myself." Agreed, self-centeredness is sin. But the ultimate in self-centeredness is undue self-protection, which is why we often avoid digging deep. I am not promoting an unhealthy, ingrown, narcissistic exercise, but rather a healthy examination of our hearts and souls for the purpose of healing and growth.

Our goal is to tear down cracked foundations and rebuild in strength and yet, run from being self-absorbed or obsessed. I want you to know who you are in God, but to get there, we have to weed through all the junk in your head that has given you a false identity. I want you to be able to clearly ask, "Who does God say that I am?" and then believe it.

PUTTING YOUR STUFF AWAY

Next, we're on to soul clutter. It's different from the noise. Soul clutter is the collection of emotional, relational, and spiritual issues we have been stepping over. Each one needs to be picked up, sorted, and put away. Clutter will stand between you and the dance with God. It can keep you tripping and stumbling for a lifetime.

I know you'd rather not. Sometimes I'd rather not. But let's dive in together and begin to change the way we live our lives.

Clutter happens when an issue begins to get in the way, when the steps of your soul are stacked with piles of emotions, thoughts, and relationships that need attention. Maybe you've been tripping over them for years now.

In the book, I gave you a list of prompts to get you thinking. I'm going to reproduce that list here and ask you to make personal notes beside each one. Respond to each idea honestly. Tell yourself and God where you are in regard to each one of these ideas. If one is a nonissue, then rejoice and move to the next one. When you find where you have accumulated clutter, then write about it. If it's clutter you've already dealt with, then recount how and when you did that soul work.

If you find this list overwhelming, then approach it the same way you'd eat an elephant, one little bite at a time. Work on a few today, then a few tomorrow.

- Numbing techniques of a hundred varieties

_____

_____

- Overscheduling yourself or your family to avoid the emptiness

_____

_____

- Gossiping

_____

_____

- Isolation

_____

_____

- Escapism with movies, novels, television, or the Internet

_____

_____

- Lying to yourself or to others

_____

_____

- Believing lies you have been told

_____

_____

- Rebellion

_____

_____

- Rejection

- Drivenness and perfectionism

- Fears

- Envy

- Legalism

- Insecurity

- Codependency

- Depression

- Anger

_____

_____

- Bitterness

_____

_____

- A critical spirit

_____

_____

- Obsessions

_____

_____

- Shopping

_____

_____

- Body image

_____

_____

- Relationships

_____

_____

- Lusts—physical and emotional

_____

_____

- Self-abuse

_____

_____

- Reckless dieting

_____

_____

- Sabotaging your health

_____

_____

- Addictions

_____

_____

- Unforgiveness

_____

_____

- Unrepentance—continuing to consciously choose a known sin

_____

_____

I imagine that some of the clutter in your soul is beginning to surface. So now what? Let's begin with baby steps.

Acknowledge the mess. You realize that it may require getting messy to get clean, and it could take a while to get things sorted out. Acknowledge the mess in prayer. It's okay to lay this big pile of clutter before the Lord and ask Him where to begin. I can't think of a better place for you to turn with your heavy load.

Realize that you may have to call for help. You and I belong to the body of Christ, and there is a reason why Scripture instructs us to carry one another's burdens.

Sometimes we can crumple underneath the weight of heaviness. You don't have to go through this alone to prove that you are superhuman or superspiritual. Can you think of three people in your life who might be safe, available, and mature enough to walk with you? You may only need one, but think of three.

Pray and seek prayer covering. If I am convinced of anything spiritually, I am convinced that nothing powerful happens in our lives apart from prayer. To begin to deal with the clutter in your soul will require power that overcomes weakness.

> *You may be asking, What if I truly don't have anyone in my life who is safe or mature enough to walk with me?*
>
> *Don't panic. I am so grateful that you realize there is no one you can trust with your heart. What a huge step of discernment and maturity. Don't connect yourself with an unhealthy person just to have a partner for your journey. Pursue God in private and pursue Him in prayer for a safe person or a healthy community of believers. And then wait for His timing and His person.*

Begin on your knees. Ask others to cover you in prayer. They don't have to know everything, but they can certainly pray for strength and wisdom.

Expect this season of reconciling, reordering, and repairing to take longer than you think it will. Life should come with a warning label: "Everything always takes longer than you think it will." It is especially true with soul work. To recognize the clutter in your life is only the beginning. To sort it all out and put it away can take a while.

> *Do you remember how to pray?*
> *P is for praise. Praise God first.*
> *R is for repent. Recount and turn*
>   *away from your sin.*
> *A is ask anything for anybody.*
> *Y is yourself. Save you until last.*
> *Backwards these letters spell*
>   *YARP, not exactly the*
>   *instruction of Jesus.*

Go ahead and begin now. To delay any longer is to allow more clutter to crowd your way. Don't put it off any longer.

Journal. I know that some of you do and some of you don't. But would you at least try? Draw pictures if you have to. Doodles and diagrams of the steps you are taking. The dreams you

I've been learning lately that God doesn't make us sit in the corner. He holds us while we go through the process of listening for the noise in our lives and dealing with the clutter we've accumulated. I always thought I was going to have to sit in the corner. I'm so relieved.

—Leigh

are dreaming. Some women love to scrapbook. Would you consider journaling the scrapbook of your soul?

Allow God to lavish you with His grace. Honestly, I have met very few people who know much about the grace of God. I am a devoted student, only beginning to learn of His incredible riches of grace. I love the following teaching from 2 Corinthians 12:9:

My grace is sufficient for you.

I love this quote by Spurgeon:

The other evening I was riding home after a heavy day's work. I felt very wearied, and sore depressed, when swiftly, and suddenly as a lightning flash, that text came to me, "My grace is sufficient for [you]." I reached home and looked it up in the original, and at last it came to me in this way, "MY grace is sufficient for [you]"; and I said, "I should think it is, Lord," and burst out laughing . . . It seemed to make unbelief so absurd. It was as though some little fish, being very thirsty, was troubled about drinking the river dry and [the Thames River] said, "Drink away, little fish, my stream is sufficient for [you]." . . . Again I imagined a man away up yonder, in a lofty mountain, saying to himself, "I breathe so many cubic feet of air every year, I fear I shall exhaust the oxygen in the atmosphere," but earth might say, "Breathe away, O man, and fill the lungs ever, my atmosphere is sufficient for [you]." Oh brethren, be great believers! Little faith will bring your souls to heaven, but great faith will bring heaven to your souls.

—C. H. Spurgeon[1]

Allow God to lavish you with His grace. Don't keep beating yourself up. Most of us are prone to guilt. So much guilt in fact that we become paralyzed by the process and choke out the good work God is doing. Let God forgive, heal, restore, soothe, mend, and strengthen. That is grace, and there is plenty of it for you and for me. You cannot drink dry the river of grace or breathe the last of God's gifts for you.

THE EYE OF THE BEHOLDER

If all that truly matters is the eye of the beholder, then why have we listened to the noise in our heads for so long? Why have we tripped over the same clutter for years? Would you make up your mind to be free of these distractions so that you can hear what the Beholder has to say about you?

It has been a scary prayer to pray, but I have learned that when I say, *Okay, God, whatever it takes. I'm ready. I want to get to work on my soul. Come and work in power for Your glory,* then God comes. And He always comes in mercy. Expect Him to be gentle and loving. Expect Him to begin healing. Expect His great joy over your new heart and desire to change.

Do you want to hear the words of the Beholder? What is He saying to you today? Sit still and listen. When you hear with your heart, then write what He has said.

Chapter Six

SOMETIMES THE PRODIGAL, SOMETIMES THE ELDER BROTHER

If there is a question attached to the soul of a woman, maybe it's "Do you think I'm beautiful?" When God answers from the depth of His great love, it makes some of us feel like the wallflower who is asked to dance. But we can become distracted from His invitation because of the other lovers, whispers of unbelief, noise and clutter, and because we are sometimes the prodigal, sometimes the elder brother.

I love this chapter. Not because it's great writing on my part or even great insight. I just know the end of the story, and I love that. I know that at the end, the God of heaven runs to hold us. I'm not over it. Maybe I never will be. I hope I never get over the truth of mercy and grace. I hope I never grow hardened to the pursuing love of God. I hope you don't either.

Maybe we should begin with the end this time. Would you close your eyes and picture the Father running to you? Not when you've gotten it all figured out and fessed up, but right now, in the midst of your life. Today—in your kitchen or at your desk or sitting on top of your bed. Wherever you are right now, imagine the God of the universe running to hold you.

I am sitting on my sofa with a laptop on my knees. I have on jeans and an old Carolina sweatshirt. No makeup and day-old hair. Books are scattered everywhere, and the dryer is running. The house is quiet because the kids are at school, but there are little reminders of them everywhere, like the popsicle stick I had to move so I could sit down. I'm sure it was William. Anyway, you have the general idea. Don't get ready to imagine. Just stop where you are and picture God. I am closing my eyes to imagine with you.

Don't go any farther until you really stop and close your eyes. I don't want you to miss this one.

Oh my.

I hadn't expected to cry. I really hadn't expected to begin weeping. I just wanted the picture in my head, but such strong emotion came with it. I imagined the Lord scooping me into His arms and my head resting on His shoulder. Right then is when the tears came. I think they are tears of relief. They feel like little-girl tears in a woman's body. Surely God must know how desperately a woman longs to be held. I forget until a moment like this. I cry because I don't have to be the strongest one anymore. I think I cry because it feels as if He whispers, "It's okay, Angela. You don't have to worry so much. I'll take it from here."

What picture do you have in your head? What does God whisper as you fall into His arms? We'll talk more about this later.

_____

_____

_____

As usual, you should probably reread this chapter in the book. I can't wait to see what God has for us.

I HAVE BEEN A PRODIGAL

Since the parable is so powerful, let's go with it and watch it unfold. Make sure you have your Bible handy and turn to Luke 15. Begin by reading verses 11–13.

Maybe you've never thought of yourself as a prodigal. Or maybe you've known the truth all along. Did you know that anytime you or I willfully choose to turn away from God even though we know better, then we are prodigals?

Sometimes we only think of prodigals as sons or daughters who have run away from home and chosen wild living. Those are definitely prodigals, but there is more to being a prodigal than just being a rebellious child. I believe that a prodigal is someone who has squandered the wealth God has given. Those of us who know better and still have chosen poorly, willfully choosing the distraction over the dance with God.

Take a few minutes and think about the wealth that you have been given because of God. What is your share of His estate? What gifts has the Father given to you?

_____

_____

_____

When we turn away from God, out of rebellion or weakness or temptation, we leave the dance and wander off into the distant country. Have you ever taken everything God has given to you and done for you and just left? Journal your thoughts.

_____

_____

_____

Where would you place yourself right now?

> At the dance in the arms of God.
> At the dance, standing in the shadows.
> Thinking about taking my inheritance and getting out of here.
> Driving off to the distant country.
> Been living out here in the faraway land for quite some time.

LIFE IN THE FARAWAY LAND

Continue reading with Luke 15:14–16.

I have a friend who says that sin "takes you farther than you ever intended to go, costs you more than you ever intended to pay, and keeps you longer than you ever intended to stay." It's the story of the prodigal.

You see, when you and I are in the presence of God, then when our supply of grace runs out, He gives more. When we are lacking forgiveness, it is ours for the asking. When we are in need of wisdom, He provides. His good gifts to us are always being replenished because He is pouring Himself into our emptiness. We are partakers of His wealth because we are daughters of the Father.

It's just that when we pack up what we have been given and drive off in search of something better, the riches come to an end. We will spend everything we brought

and begin to be in need. Like the prodigal, we can find ourselves empty and broke, feeding pigs in a sty.

If you've ever found yourself in a faraway land, turning from God, describe where you ended up:

_____

_____

_____

Can you specifically describe what called (or continues to call) you away from the dance with God? Addictions? Obsessions? Curiosity?

_____

_____

This could be a key place to really do some thinking. To begin realizing what tempts you to leave the arms of God could be a huge step toward change. To know where you might be tripped can help you be prepared the next time. Are you willing to ask a close friend what she sees? I've done this. I've given a couple of people I respect permission to say the hard things. I hate it, but the work it does in my soul is worth it. If you can't let someone in, can you at least be honest with yourself about temptation? In what ways do you or your friend see you turning away from God?

_____

_____

Maybe you have wandered away like the prodigal sometime in your past. Maybe you are far away from God right now. Maybe you feel the allure of the distant country and are considering a trip there soon. Wherever you are, read what Jesus says in Luke 15:17–20.

My favorite phrase in that passage is, _When he came to his senses._ Do you see the application for your own life? Whatever has distracted you. Wherever it has taken you. No matter how long you've been away. The lesson is that you and I can come to our senses.

Do you remember a time of "coming to your senses"? Describe it here.

_____

_____

Eugene Peterson implies in his paraphrase of this passage that the lowliness of the pigsty brought the prodigal to his senses. How far will you have to go until you "come to your senses"? What would it look like in your life to "come to your senses" right now, no more delays?

_____

_____

Write out a prayer of returning.

_____

_____

Coming to your senses might mean:

- turning from repetitive, plaguing sin or foolish living.
- turning or running from an unhealthy relationship.
- becoming awake to the life and possibilities ahead of you. Dreaming again.
- beginning new habits that improve your life.
- refocusing on your family.
- making a new commitment to spiritual passion.
- seeking counseling or professional help for emotional wounds.
- regaining or forging a sense of order and purpose for living.

PRODIGALS LIKE YOU AND ME

I am guessing that you are probably not a typical prodigal. You're probably not like my friend Rob who kept being called away into his life of drugs and alcohol addiction. One jail cell to another. One rehab and then the next.

The whole idea here is for you to ask yourself honestly:

Are you hiding sin that distracts you from God? What is that sin, and where does it take you in secret?

_____

_____

Do you live separate lives? One that you live in front of your family and one in secret? You realize that you can either actually live a secret life or you can just be planning one in your head. Both are incredibly dangerous. Truthfully, if you live or plan separate lives, what are they? What does the secret life seem to offer that your heart longs for?

_____

_____

What if someone could pull up the history on your computer, collect the receipts from your credit card, or know everything that you've seen on television. What would they find? Would you be okay with that? I completely understand privacy, but beyond that, is there a behavior or pattern that you want to keep hidden?

_____

_____

Do you hear the voice of God calling you back to the dance and still refuse to answer?

_____

_____

Your ordinary, run-of-the-mill prodigal can be a woman like you or me. She is a woman whose heart is becoming harder. She is squandering her life and all the riches God has given to her. She probably knows that she is not dancing, but has decided at some level that she doesn't care anymore. She may be living openly or secretly, but either way, there is an ever-growing distance between her and the Father.

What is certain is that eventually, the allure runs out. The distant country and its emptiness begin to stink like a pigsty. The prodigal will always, ultimately, find herself longing to go home.

WATCHING FOR OUR RETURN

Now read Luke 15:20. You might want to underline this one in your Bible. *The Message* paraphrases Jesus' words like this:

> When he was still a long way off, his father saw him. His heart pounding, he ran out, embraced him, and kissed him.

This is where we began. Remember imagining God running to you, embracing you, and kissing you? What was your response to the picture of God running to you? Did you want to run toward Him or run away from His embrace?

I think that sometimes we believe we can only allow ourselves to be embraced by God when we have decided we are pure enough or repentant enough. There is nothing in this parable that tells us that the son came home with pure motives and a pure heart. He came home intending to live as a servant to get away from the pigsty and pig food. He came home because he had nowhere else to go.

Maybe you can get to the place of understanding that God calls you beautiful and even enter into His embrace. But then the whispers start: *You'll never stay pure enough. You can't hold it all together. You're going to lose the embrace of God.*

What I want to say to you here is that even if we don't understand a holy God running toward a self-centered, manipulative, sinful woman—even if you can't figure that one out—it is still true. God still runs. I hear you protesting, "But you don't know me." I don't have to. I know the Father heart of God, and He will run to hold you.

GOING HOME

Hope you've still got that Bible open. Read Luke 15:21–24. Make sure you hear the son saying to his father, "I am no longer worthy" (v. 21).

No longer worthy. How many lives have stayed locked down in this one? I have a friend whose father told her growing up, "You are a stupid idiot, and you'll never be worth anything." If her dad weren't dead, I'd want to hit him. Can you imagine what that does to the soul? She heard it all her life. Now he's gone, and it's still all she can hear.

Most of us didn't hear those words growing up but remain stuck in the land of *no longer worthy*.

Here's the deal, and I hope it comes as a huge relief for you: You were not worthy, even when you thought maybe you were. Becoming worthy of the Father doesn't have anything to do with your performance. You can't get good enough. Look cute enough. Act pure enough. We have been made worthy of the Father's love because we ask Jesus to cover us with His forgiveness. Jesus makes us lovely to the Father. Jesus covers our sin. Jesus is the only reason that the Father runs to us. Through Jesus, we belong to God.

If you still feel "no longer worthy," would you ask yourself these questions from the chapter:

Do you feel guilty?

> **Have you been unable to clean your slate?**
> **Do you feel you've offended God?**
> **Have you abused others?**
> **Do you carry anger and judgment?**
> **Do you harbor unforgiveness?**
> **Have you looked to counterfeit sources for intimacy?**

Do you feel shame?

> **Have you been abused?**
> > **Disgraced?**
> > **Dishonored?**
> > **Humiliated?**
> > **Exposed?**
> > **Accused?**
> > **Spit on?**

Because of guilt and shame, we can decide that we are not worthy of the Father's arms and run away in our embarrassment.

How is the Holy Spirit prompting you to deal with these ideas about worth, guilt, and shame?

_____

_____

_____

I realize that the world assigns value to a woman for many reasons—her aptitude, her skills, her body, or her overall life performance. When the Father runs to hold you, when He invites you to dance the dance of your life in His arms, it is not about your performance; it's about your identity. He runs to you because you belong to Him. And you belong to Him because you have believed in Jesus as His Son. That's it. End of discussion. When you belong to Jesus, then you are worthy to the Father.

You can protest. Lament your sin. Wallow in your choices. Choose to continue in unbelief. Waffle in and out of believing. Doesn't matter what you do—that's not the point. The point is, the blood of Jesus covers your heart and makes you beautiful to the Father.

Now that, my sister, is something to throw a party about. It's what the Father did, and it's good reason for you to celebrate His goodness for the rest of your life.

Let's run with that for a minute. Would you say that your life is woven with threads of celebration? What and how do you celebrate? Are you on the lookout for the smallest victories that need a celebration or party?

_____

_____

Take a few minutes and look around your life and your family. Who needs a victory party soon? Could you plan something small or even large in the next few weeks? What about a batch of cookies (baked or bought) or some flowers (grown or purchased) that would celebrate a friendship? Life is much too short. Dance the happy dance with someone today.

_____

_____

Are you making a big deal about the goodness of God? Don't you think it's time? What about a gathering of people you love just to celebrate the blessings of God? I can assure you that after a bowl of ice cream shared with friends who talk about the great gifts of God, no one will leave lonely or miserable or discouraged. What can you do to celebrate God?

I HAVE BEEN THE ELDER BROTHER

Here's where it could get a little uncomfortable. We're going to talk about the "good one," the one who stayed home. Sometimes we have been the prodigal. But then sometimes we can be the elder brother.

Read Luke 15:25–32. This may not apply to some of you. I kind of wish it didn't apply so completely to me. We elder brother types are fairly gross.

I actually talked to an elder brother woman on the phone the other day. I had not heard someone be so blatantly the elder brother in a while. I heard my old legalism. I heard haughtiness that made me shudder. I heard judgment, "in the name of Jesus," that scared me. I heard a woman in ministry being the snotty elder brother. I remembered my own years there, and I ached. My words to her fell on deaf ears. I just wanted to get off the phone. Elder brothers are self-righteous, and you can't really tell them anything. One day, they just get whacked over the head with their own piety. Maybe that's how they come to their senses.

If you feel there is an outside shot that your life falls under the heading of elder brother, please don't wait until you get whacked. If you hear God speaking to you in these pages, don't harden your heart. Allow yourself to be tender and receive direction from the Holy Spirit. Believe me, you don't want to live any longer in haughtiness. It's a prison everyone else can see, but you don't even know you're in.

With that in mind, let's work through some of these thoughts about the elder brother.

The prodigal knew he was a sinner.
The elder brother could not see his own sinfulness.

Do you have eyes to see inside of your own heart, or can you just see what's wrong with everyone else? What elder brother traits can you see in your own heart?

_____

_____

Are you "religious" for the sake of appearance? Does keeping the "rules" make you feel safe? What religious rules make you feel safe?

_____

_____

How do you respond when someone blows it and breaks a rule? Do you offer a heart of compassion or a heart of judgment? If judgment, what is it that sends you immediately to that response instead of grace? Where did that come from? Are you afraid of extending grace? Why would that be true?

_____

_____

_____

The elder brother thought the father loved him because he was hardworking and faithful.

Have you believed that obedience earns you the Father's love? Write what you know about receiving the Father's love. How does it come to us, and why?

_____

_____

Do you understand that obedience is our gift back to God for His love? How does your life reflect your gift of obedience? How do you desire to give more in this area?

Because the elder brother had not known grace, he was not able to extend grace.
Do you know a woman who knows something about living and giving grace? As I mentioned earlier, do whatever you can to get close to her. I can write to you

about it, but I'm not sure if you can get "living in grace" until you bump up against someone who has it and it rubs off on you.

I just know that you cannot give what you do not have. Pray about this one. Ask God for more.

He gives you everything, His lavish gifts and His holy love, because you belong to Him.

Write out your prayer for a friend and giver of grace.

_____
_____
_____
_____
_____

I want to recommend *The Ragamuffin Gospel* by Brennan Manning if you haven't read it. But even more, find that woman who radiates grace. She'll probably change your life.

The elder brother was bound by unforgiveness.

When you come to understand how much you have already been forgiven by the Father, then you want to give that to someone else. The elder-brother-type woman doesn't get it. She holds on to unforgiveness, and it keeps her locked in a cage from the inside out. She has the key for escape . . . to begin forgiving.

You cannot impart what you do not possess.

Do you have a list? What if you just began forgiving everyone you could think of for no good reason except that you have been forgiven in Jesus? What if they don't deserve it and you just forgive them anyway? How cool would that be? How do you think it would feel to be released from grudge bondage? It would feel wonderful. So wonderful, in fact, you might get to dancing.

So go ahead. Write about it. Pray about it. Journal. But don't stop there. Forgive every one of them and be free.

The elder brother didn't know that he had always possessed the riches of the father. We talked about this earlier . . . the riches of the father. They belonged to both the prodigal and to his brother. We are also partakers because we belong to God.

Have you said thank you lately? Remember God's blessings to you and write about His lavish gifts. Write out a prayer of praise to Him.

The elder brother didn't hear the music with his heart.
He didn't know he'd been invited to the dance.

Are you missing the music and the celebration of life? What happened?

Does anything make you laugh anymore? How can you begin to return to laughter and a joyful heart?

THE WAY OF THE ELDER BROTHER

Okay, how about it? Have you been the elder brother? Do you find yourself struggling with his demeanor? How and why?

Did you realize that underneath the self-righteousness is usually a woman fueled by fear, pain, and sorrow?

See if any of these fears belong to you. Circle them and elaborate beside those that apply.

- Rejection

- Betrayal

- Exposure

- Abandonment

- More pain

- Insecurities

- Consequences of sin

We'll talk more about our fears in the chapter called "His Perfect Love." But until then, make notes on the ideas that seem to press into your heart. If you realize that underneath your attitude is a spirit of fear, then begin taking it to God in prayer.

Pain and sorrow. They can fuel the same elder-brother attitude. Take a look at the list and see if any of the items apply. Again, circle and elaborate.

- Coping with losses and disappointment

_____

- Bearing sufferings

_____

- Making sacrifices

_____

- Enduring physical affliction

_____

- Enduring mental anguish

_____

- Allowing bitterness to grow

_____

- Scars from divorce or broken relationships

_____

- Loneliness

_____

Ask yourself how these circumstances have shaped your heart and your attitude toward others. It's easy to let pain and sorrow begin to stir up anger inside of us, and like the elder brother, we can quickly get downright mad at everybody.

If you know that you are an angry woman (and if you're not sure about it, ask someone who lives with you), then begin, in earnest, to find the beginning and do whatever it takes to untangle that thread from your life. We say it all the time, but it's still true: Life is too short.

WHAT'S A PRODIGAL/ELDER-BROTHER KIND OF GIRL TO DO?

Whether you are the prodigal who has wandered away from the dance or the elder brother who can't hear the music, it's a miserable place either way. Both keep us separate from God and the dance He has for our lives.

Over and over again, the same will be true. When there are distractions. When the world tries to cut in. When we trip over our two left feet and feel frustrated. The answer is always and only *Jesus*. The answer will always be,

Return to the arms of God.

Is there a returning that still needs to happen in your life? Have you been dragging your heart for all these pages? Isn't it amazing that inside the tight embrace of God is where your life will finally be free? That doesn't quite go together except that it's God. Can you hear Him saying to you, "In My arms you will be free"?

I want you to know the freedom that Christ can bring to your life. I want you to live the message of Galatians 5:1:

You have been set free for freedom's sake.

I want you to hear God call you beautiful. I want you to rejoice in His lavish gifts. I want you to dance!

Chapter Seven

A DESPERATE
AND PURSUING HEART

*If there is a question attached to the soul of a woman, maybe it's
"Do you think I'm beautiful?" When God answers from the depth of
His great love, it makes some of us feel like the wallflower who is
asked to dance. But we can become distracted from His invitation
because of the other lovers, whispers of unbelief, noise and clutter,
and because we are sometimes the prodigal, sometimes the elder
brother. To return to the music and strong embrace of God
requires a desperate and pursuing heart.*

We've been talking about hearing God call you beautiful and dancing in His
arms. I bet you realize by now that the world isn't really cooperating with this
whole idea. If it involves your heart and God, then a battle will likely ensue. The
battle is for your soul, and if Satan can't have your soul, he'll settle for ruining your
entire life. He'd love for you to be miserable from now until heaven. He'd love for
you never to dance. And he'd love for you to keep missing the invitation of God. Of
course, I'm not telling most of you anything new.

The question is, What are you going to do about it? Remain the same?
Dreaming about dancing, but never really moving your feet? I know you're almost
too tired to fight. Too old to care so much anymore. And too accustomed to the
life you've known to get excited about changing. A friend said to me the other day,
"I've already started over twice in my life. I'm forty-seven years old, and I don't
think I have the energy to do it again." I understand, and yet, there is so much left
to live. I felt like screaming, "You are too wonderful to quit. Please don't let your
heart die this young. There is dancing ahead. God is still on the throne and able

to move heaven and earth to redeem your life. Don't stand in the shadows. Just call His name."

I don't think you want to stay there in the shadows, hanging around the edge of your life watching. I believe you understand by now that every distraction imaginable will come to lure you away from the arms of God. But this chapter is about wanting Him more than you want anything else. There is a conscious choosing ahead. You will have to decide, "Do I want to dance the dance of my life, or do I just want to keep shuffling around like this?"

If you haven't reread this chapter in the book, this would be a good time before we dive in.

Keep in mind that I believe these next pages to be pivotal. A hinge, so to speak. If you decide to apply the message of this book to your life, this is the place where you will turn in that direction. Or not.

THE CHURCH LADY

I hope I didn't offend you with this section of the book. Well, maybe I hope I ruffled your feathers a little. I love the church. I grew up in church. I can't remember not being around the church and church gatherings and church people. It just took me way too long to realize that becoming a "church lady" doesn't mean that I know squat about the heart and passion of God.

I grew up going to youth group, potlucks, homecoming, gospel singing under revival tents, committee meetings, bake sales, car washes, retreats, conferences, and any other spiritual-sounding activity that was advertised in the church bulletin. I loved all that. Absolutely loved it. I had a place and felt loved and accepted. I loved the people and the hubbub and the routine. I was good at doing church.

The church lady has a good heart. She is drawn to God and wants to serve Him out of gratitude. She wants to learn more about the One who has saved her. It's just that over time, more serving and more learning may become a checklist or a substitute for deeper passion . . . a doing instead of becoming.

What about you? What was your introduction into church? Did you grow up there or come to church later in life?

_____

_____

_____

_____

_____

_____

I want you to hear my heart. I love church. I still love church. I just missed the whole point of God for many years. Somehow I loved becoming the church lady and mistook that for becoming godly. But good grief, it feels so good to be in the "church club"—to hang out with your friends, bring food to the sick, make care packages for the refugees, and teach children's church. It can get to feeling so good that it becomes the substitute for a passionate pursuit of God.

Hear me on this one. It is fabulous to serve and give and sacrifice. It is a part of the calling for every believer. But service and doing is not a relationship with God. It doesn't get us closer to the mark. Sometimes it becomes the curtain that we hide behind, pretending that we know what we're talking about.

Every Sunday morning moms and dads all across the country hand their babies across half doors to the same people. The good people who work in the nursery. What I've seen is that everywhere I go there are people serving in a hundred places in the church. They may never make it to the service, but they've "been to church." I have come to realize that some people are hiding in nurseries and classrooms and kitchens. Some of them have hidden for years.

How about you? Have you become a proper church lady? Theologically educated? Hospitable? Quiet and gentle? Hiding and incredibly empty? How did it happen and how does it make you feel?

_____

_____

_____

_____

_____

_____

_____

_____

_____

_____

_____

_____

_____

_____

_____

_____

_____

_____

_____

_____

_____

_____

_____

_____

Being the church lady touches my need for a sense of belonging, at least a pseudo-sense of belonging. I think I found some kind of safety in the structure.

—Nancy

What avenues have you taken in your walk with Christ that could be labeled "church lady"?

_____

_____

Doesn't it make sense that _doing_ is not _becoming_? All of us are doing like crazy. Very few of us are becoming. I told you that my counselor is booked solid with Christian women who are dying on the inside. Service and hospitality are not cutting it. So many are smiling and limping along on Prozac. Hearts are broken and lives are hurting, and we just keep signing up for one more thing, hoping we'll stumble into healing and passion.

Now, whom can you tell? When you get the church-lady groove going, it seems as if you have it all together. And after a few years of pretending, we decide it's probably better not to find out any different. We meet with other women, but nothing powerful happens because we're all just smiling.

Let's talk about small groups. You know, little groups of women who meet together for Bible study or prayer or fellowship. I hope you are in one of those right now. So first, would you write down every good thing you can think of about belonging to a small group of women?

_____

_____

What is your heart's desire in regard to a small group? What would your dream group be, and how would you relate to one another?

_____

_____

Now, what are the pitfalls of this kind of connectedness? How have you been burned in the past? What makes you hesitant with these women?

_____

_____

THE UNCHURCH LADY

Becoming unchurch. I wish I could make a quick list, ten easy steps, but I can't. There is no such list. Becoming unchurch is about laying down pretense and facades. It's about stepping outside the lines you have drawn around your spirituality and seeing what God has for you out there. I promise that He has more for you than you could imagine. If you have somehow wrangled your spirituality into categories with neat little answers for every situation imaginable, then hang on— God is probably getting ready to blow the doors off that one.

A healthy small group:
- *rejoices over victories.*
- *prays and mourns over defeats.*
- *keeps confidences.*
- *carries one another's burdens.*
- *encourages passion.*
- *forgives quickly.*
- *restores often.*

I can't just package this idea into some structure, where one size fits all. As my pastor would say, this kind of change requires a "paradigm shift." Your framework for thinking and feeling may need a demolition and reconstruction. All of the strong, essential elements of your faith still there, just rearranged to reflect more clearly the heart of God.

Sometimes it's easier to remain the church lady because we're afraid of what the unchurch lady might be. Are you afraid? If so, why?

_____

_____

_____

_____

I have a godly friend who says she wants to become dangerous. Not your typical church-lady aspiration. Some of us might initially think she's stepped across the line of freedom and into rebellion. But God knows her heart. He knows that she lived timidly for too many years. He knows that she lived under strict interpretations of doctrine that did not reflect the Father's merciful intentions. He knows that she desires to glorify Him with every word from her mouth and every step in

I was raised to believe that being a godly woman was about being a total servant and all those things my mom is. I was taught to aspire to Bible studies, missionary meetings, and Vacation Bible School. I still love all that, but I realize that I don't hear the passion of the bridegroom for the bride there. I will not find out who I am in Christ in only those pursuits.

—Cindy

her journey. I think He loves that she wants to be dangerous. She is saying, "I want to be strong in the name of Jesus. I want wisdom and the courage to take God-sized risks where very few will. I want to speak up in confidence when I have something to say. I want to be vulnerable and transparent. I want my life to draw others into this adventure that is life in Christ."

Come to think of it, she makes me want to be dangerous too.

What would you look like as an unchurch lady? What would your attributes be?

_____

_____

_____

Who in your life would be threatened if you became unchurch?

_____

_____

_____

Does becoming "unchurch" seem like becoming "un-christian" to you? What makes you struggle with this idea?

_____

_____

_____

Moving from church lady into unchurch doesn't happen without a "want to." Most of us try every other spiritual endeavor before we get there. Becoming unchurch requires becoming desperate. Just the thought of it is enough to scare most of us away.

POOR IN SPIRIT

I guess I always thought that desperation was to be avoided at any cost. Now I am learning that being desperate isn't always a reflection of a disaster, but an attitude that is cultivated. Desperation for God is a good thing.

Read the following definition of _desperate_:

_____

_____

_____

_____

_____

_____

_____

_____

_____

_____

_____

_____

_____

_____

_____

Actually, I'm afraid of passion, both spiritually with God and physically with my husband.

— an honest woman

Sometimes I think I want to become a nun to get away from every temptation and be disciplined. Then I think I'll be a woman who is pleasing to God. But that is not the woman God thought of in me—living in passion as a mother, wife, friend, is no less holy than the monastery.

— Martha

Involving or employing extreme measures in an attempt to escape defeat or frustration.

If you became desperate for God, I mean really decided to go for it, do you understand what that could mean for the rest of your life? It might mean that you get extreme, willing to do anything or fight any battle to escape the pitiful way you have been wandering through life. It means that you decide the fight is worth it. Why should frustration and confusion keep winning when life in Christ offers a light for your feet and purpose for your days?

To become desperate for God probably means that you begin to live in the victory that has been promised to you in Jesus Christ.

> Every God-begotten person conquers the world's ways.
> The conquering power that brings the world to its knees is our faith.
> The person who wins out over the world's ways is simply the one
> who believes Jesus is the Son of God. (1 John 5:4–5 THE MESSAGE)

I told you we'd get here . . . we've arrived at the hinge. Here is the place where this whole idea turns. Here is where you will have to turn your life in order to change and become, or you can choose not to turn with these thoughts and remain where you are. The choice is yours. Right now, I am fervently praying that you are overcome with great courage and desire. I am asking God to make you hungry for Him, consumed with a craving for His power and passion.

Let's walk through the steps in this turning.

> Blessed are the poor in spirit,
> For theirs is the kingdom of heaven. (Matthew 5:3 NKJV)

Remember that the kingdom of heaven means being near to the presence of God. The presence of God is what you and I have been talking about since the beginning of this book. To be in the presence of God is to be dancing in His arms. That's where the riches of His gifts are. That's where our hearts long to be.

What do you believe the Father has waiting for you in His presence? What is missing from your life? What does your heart crave?

Remember that the kingdom, the presence of God, is a blessing that comes to the poor in spirit. Poverty of spirit comes to us after we have tried on our own and come to realize that we cannot be enough.

We have looked inside our souls and truly seen that nothing good is there. When we have owned up to our sin and fessed up to our motives. When we have stumbled for the hundredth time with the habit or pattern we thought we had beaten. When we have yelled and cursed and screamed like a bratty little baby. When we've finally let the truth of our insides out, into the light comes the reality of poverty.

Understanding our own poverty means we finally realize that apart from God, we cannot do anything purposeful, strong, eternal, good, righteous, or holy. We realize that we cannot fill ourselves with achievements. We cannot manipulate relationships to make us whole. We come to see our emptiness for what it truly is: the absence of God.

Without Me you can do nothing. (John 15:5 NKJV)

I have a friend in my life right now who knows God. She has been saved and set apart for all eternity. I truly believe that she belongs to the Father and, at one point, gave herself to Him fully. Now, though, she walks at a distance. Her life is truly a mess. Her soul is a mess. She frets and worries like no one I've ever met. Her relationships at every turn are strained and difficult. Her career is suffering. Her marriage ended three years ago. She is spinning like a top, on the phone all the time with anyone who will listen, e-mailing, whining, becoming more and more the victim of "an awful life."

Right off the bat, I knew my place in her life: take her back to Jesus. And I did. And she politely went with me. But then, doggone it, she turned right around and wandered away. I was a little dismayed, but trying to be faithful, I got right back in there, interacted for days and took her by the hand, back to Jesus. "Stay here and don't move again," I firmly instructed. She nodded her tear-stained face in agreement. And then, to beat everything, she wandered away again. So frustrated. I am at this moment still so frustrated with this woman. She knows better. She is lost with a map in her pocket. It makes no sense to me. But then I finally realized, she's not desperate yet. She feels desperate about her circumstances, but she's not desperate for Jesus. She still thinks she can figure this one out. There is no poverty of spirit about her.

Do you truly realize that apart from Jesus, you can do nothing? How do you know this to be true?

Where are you in regard to desperate? Are you like my friend who keeps wandering in and out of the presence of God, or are you ready to do whatever it takes to get to Him?

If you aren't ready, what do you think it will take to make you crave God?

Are you afraid of being desperate? Take a few minutes and consider your fears. What are you afraid of?

I am personally finding great comfort and peace in my "desperateness" for God. I feel I finally have "the answer" that continues to feed my soul.

_____
_____
_____
_____
_____
_____
_____
_____
_____
_____
_____
_____
_____
_____
_____
_____

I used to have thoughts that I wanted to squish because you get so trained as the church lady to cut thoughts off right away. But the desperate woman gives permission to float those thoughts a little longer and ask the Lord what's behind this.

The church lady thinks, "I'm tired," and then she gives herself the pat answer, "Do not become weary in doing well." I am learning to let questions rise to the surface and ask Jesus, "Why am I tired, spiritually and emotionally?" I am following a little longer with the thoughts that come to mind.

— Sheila

Write out a prayer asking God to make you desperate for His presence.

_____

_____

_____

_____

_____

_____

_____

Remember that real poverty is not polite. Starving people charge the grain truck to get the food that will take away the pain of their hunger. Are you ready to charge the grain truck so that you can live the rest of your days in the presence of God? This is the hinge. Here is the turn you've been waiting for.

If you are hungry and you are ready to admit your desperation, then sign and date underneath this statement:

I'm ready to do whatever it takes to get to Jesus.

Name: _____ Date: _____

EAT, SLEEP, DRINK, BREATHE

I imagine this is all feeling a little radical to you right about now. I hope so.

Mediocre hasn't cut it. A casual glance toward God will not fill the emptiness. A Sunday pursuit will leave us feeling indifferent by Tuesday.

I believe that we are supposed to live every day in desperate pursuit of the only One who can give the food that will fill our empty souls. I call it learning to eat, sleep, drink, and breathe Jesus. If I knew of an easier way that worked, I'd surely offer it. But this is the only way I know.

How would it look if you decided to eat, sleep, drink, and breathe Jesus? Very practically, where could you begin? Can you think of five areas? Remember, we are charging the grain truck. I want to let you go slow, but my heart tells me that you just need to take off running, hard and fast after Jesus.

1. _____
2. _____
3. _____
4. _____
5. _____

This desperate pursuit is more a state of your mind than anything. When you get hungry, the desire for food is consuming. It infiltrates every thought and everything you do.

Now, what might keep you from remaining desperate for God? Go ahead and think through the obstacles so you can head them off at the pass.

_____

_____

Do you know a woman who is desperate for God? What is her name and how can you get some time with her?

_____

_____

HIS GREAT DELIGHT

What does God do with a desperate woman?

I love this.

He picks her up into the arms of His presence.

He quiets her heart with gentle love songs.

He feeds her empty soul with the bounty of His love.

Yahoo! Yes. That is exactly where I want to spend my entire life. Right there in the arms of God. I have been a million other places, but nothing, and I mean nothing, fills my longing, speaks to every desire, calms my spirit, and gives me courage like the presence of God.

Can you hear God singing over you? Listen again to the music of His words from this passage in Song of Songs:

> How beautiful you are, my darling!
>> Oh, how beautiful!
>> Your eyes behind your veil are doves,
> Your hair is like a flock of goats.
>> descending from Mount Gilead.
> Your teeth are like a flock of sheep just shorn,
>> coming up from the washing.
> Each has its twin;
>> not one of them is alone.
> Your lips are like a scarlet ribbon;
>> your mouth is lovely.
> Your temples behind your veil
>> are like the halves of a pomegranate.
> Your neck is like the tower of David,
>> built with elegance;
> on it hang a thousand shields,
>> all of them shields of warriors.
> Your two breasts are like two fawns,
>> like twin fawns of a gazelle
>> that browse among the lilies.
> Until the day breaks
>> and the shadows flee,
> I will go to the mountain of myrrh
>> and to the hill of incense.
> All beautiful you are, my darling;
>> there is no flaw in you.
>
> . . . .
>
> You have stolen my heart, my sister, my bride;
>> you have stolen my heart
> with one glance of your eyes,
>> with one jewel of your necklace.

I'm doing the church-lady thing because I don't want to be desperate. I have become fine with serving and working because I'm afraid of the deeper places.

— Lauren

How delightful is your love, my sister, my bride!
How much more pleasing is your love than wine,
and the fragrance of your perfume than any spice!
(4:1–7, 9–10)

God sees the desperate woman charging the grain truck and calls her beautiful.

If you are still struggling with this truth, write out your prayers of longing. And if you are beginning to believe the truth of Scripture, then write a prayer of gratefulness.

_____

_____

_____

God sees your emptiness,
He knows you can't do this alone,
He loves that you have come running to Him,
And He calls you beautiful,

NEAR THE KINGDOM

Tell me again, what is the hinge upon which your whole life could turn?

_____

_____

Look around and see if anyone is willing to charge the grain truck with you. There is so much more strength when we band together. With whom will you go? How will you begin?

_____

_____

I can't wait to meet you and see a new woman, desperate and dancing the dance of her life in the arms of God!

Chapter Eight

THE ONLY HOPE WE HAVE

If there is a question attached to the soul of a woman, maybe it's "Do you think I'm beautiful?" When God answers from the depth of His great love, it makes some of us feel like the wallflower who is asked to dance. But we can become distracted from His invitation because of the other lovers, whispers of unbelief, noise and clutter, and because we are sometimes the prodigal, sometimes the elder brother. To return to the music and strong embrace of God requires a desperate and pursuing heart. And when a woman chooses to remain in His arms of devotion, God gives the only hope we have.

This was the very first chapter I wrote for this book. Maybe because it was the most personal and I had to get it out of me before I could do anything else. Maybe because I needed to be reminded where my hope was before I could begin. Maybe because the earth was shaking underneath me in those days, and I had no other option but to write these words.

I put this chapter in this order for a reason. I want you to understand that being a desperate, free, and passionate woman doesn't guarantee that everything will now be glorious. It's a real world that we dance in, with dangers and enemies and evil lurking. I want you to know that dancing in the arms of God will not insulate you from the winds of the journey, nor will it prevent you from the hurricanes that can come into your life and tear down everything you have built.

Here is where a lot of us can begin to stumble. We think we get it. We hear God inviting us to dance. The music is wonderful, and we feel beautiful in His arms. Then a big gust of wind blows through our lives and we begin to doubt God. The mountains we had built on begin to crumble into the sea, and we don't know what happened. Where did He go? We thought we were dancing.

I wish I could tell you that the arms of God would keep you from every awful thing. But Scripture doesn't teach that. I wish I could promise you that grieving and sorrow would not taunt you while He has you. But Scripture says it isn't so. We have the promise of heaven, but until then, this journey, this amazing adventure we live, is beset with trials and weeping that come from a fallen world.

I only know this: In the middle of a great wind, the safest place is deep inside the strongest shelter. When a particularly threatening storm blows into our neighborhood, the authorities will advise us to take our families into a room with no windows until danger has passed. Sometimes God will ask us to wait in the dark while He protects.

The only safe place we have is the tight embrace of His love. And the deeper we go, the more we are hidden from ravaging winds. Although we do not know what lies ahead, the strength of His protection makes the outcome certain. What may affect you, cannot have you. What may wound you, cannot destroy you. What may spin you around, cannot carry you away. You and I belong to God. He is our certain refuge.

Again, have you reread this chapter lately? It will help you be familiar with the path we'll take in the next pages.

Would you journal as much as you can about the storms that have come into your own life? Think about the surprise of their arrival. Your heart during and after that season. Your response to God and to others. Any lessons that you have learned.

I wrote to you that when my sister died, my daddy told me not to blame myself, but I still did. Is God bringing to mind any devastating thoughts or episodes that continue to wander around in your heart? How have you blamed yourself through the years?

The LORD is close to the brokenhearted

and saves those who are crushed in spirit. (Psalm 34:18)

Are you discovering any wounds from the past that have never found healing? What are they?

_____

_____

_____

For some of you, right this moment is the most intense storm you have ever known. Did you know that you can find real shelter in the depth of God's love? Maybe you'd like to pray and ask Him for that protection.

COMING TO KNOW HIM

How have you known God, or know Him now, as the following? Write about how God is filling these roles in your life.

Your Father. "I will be a Father to you, and you shall be My sons and daughters, says the LORD Almighty" (2 Corinthians 6:18 NKJV).

_____

_____

_____

Your Provider. "Tell them to go after God, who piles on all the riches we could ever manage" (1 Timothy 6:17 THE MESSAGE).

_____

_____

Your Mercy. "In his love and mercy he redeemed them" (Isaiah 63:9).

_____

_____

Your Shelter. "God is a safe place to hide, ready to help when we need him" (Psalm 46:1 THE MESSAGE).

_____

_____

Your Hope. "May the God of hope fill you with all joy and peace as you trust in him, so that you may overflow with hope by the power of the Holy Spirit" (Romans 15:13).

_____

_____

RAIN AND HURRICANES

Jesus said,

> [God] sends rain on the righteous and the unrighteous. (Matthew 5:45)

The idea here is that there are no exemptions. Life comes to all of us and one thing is for sure: It just keeps coming, whether we are ready or not.

I don't know what constitutes rain or a hurricane in your life right now, but God does. Do you understand that sometimes we are suffering the consequences of our choices and then sometimes we are suffering just because we are among the living? If rain falls on both the just and the unjust, then we must expect to get wet and even drenched sometimes.

What is God saying to you about any difficulty or sorrow you are facing in your life? Stop and ask for His perspective. Are you facing consequences of rain that has fallen?

_____

_____

_____

_____

Now ask for God's directive. Are you to wait for His rescue? Is there a point of action He is prompting you to take? Should you involve someone else in the process?

_____

_____

_____

_____

Although we may prefer it, we shall never attain to the fullest fruit-bearing by having all sunshine and no rain. God puts the one over against the other, the dark day of cloud and tempest against the bright day of sunshine and calm; and when the two influences work together in the soul, as they do in the natural world, they produce the greatest degree of fertility, and the best condition of heart and life.

—Charles Spurgeon[1]

TENDER MERCY

Remember the Psalm 46 passage?

> God is our refuge and strength,
>   an ever-present help in trouble.
> Therefore we will not fear, though the earth give way
>   and the mountains fall into the heart of the sea,
> though its waters roar and foam
>   and the mountains quake with their surging. (vv. 1–3)

The writer is being pounded by unrelenting wind and rains. Now look down at verse 10 in this same chapter:

> Be still, and know that I am God.

The answer from above the clouds is *Be still. Do not fret and wring your hands with worry. Lean deeper into Me and feel My strength.*

How is God trying to speak to you? Have you been still enough to hear His strong voice? Find a way to settle yourself in these next moments . . . listen to Him speak. What is He saying?

I want to tell you a story of God's tender mercy to me. It's so outside my theological box that I almost hesitate, but I know it was God and I know you are supposed to hear about it.

An event had arisen in my life that took me completely by surprise. As all hurricanes usually do, they make us afraid and worry us with their impending damage and pain. My hurricane had blown ashore, and the next morning I had a serious meeting with a lot of people to assess the damage. My heart had been racing. My mind envisioning a million scenarios. And yet, I had been praying, asking God for mercy, protection, and safety.

The night before my meeting, all the children were off to baths and the rest of homework. I had not told them anything about my next day and the anxiety it held for me. I was loading the dishwasher and clearing the table after dinner. Anna Grace, my five-year-old, twirled her way into the kitchen. And completely out of the blue, she said, "Mama, I know where God is."

"You do? Where is He, baby?" For some reason, I stopped and bent down to be at her eye level so I could really hear her answer.

"He's right above your head," she offered with authority.

"Really?"

"Yep, right there over your head."

Being a systematic theologian wanna-be, quick to recognize a teachable moment, I began to give Anna Grace a preschool lesson in God's omnipresence. "Isn't it cool, Anna Grace? God can be everywhere at the same time. He is here with us and yet, He's with other people all over the world right this minute. Did you know that about God?"

She wasn't the least bit impressed and answered, "Yeah, Mom, but I know where the angels are too."

Thinking that I was indulging my daughter, I said, "Okay, baby, where are they?"

"They are all around you in a circle, holding hands, and they're singing."

Right about then, I realized who was teaching and who was learning. "Well, what are they singing?" The words stumbled out of my mouth.

"They're singing, *Protect this girl, protect this girl.*"

Big tears in my eyes. No words. Chill bumps from head to toe. All I could ask was, "Do you really see the angels, Anna Grace?"

"No, I can't see them, but I know they're there, and I can hear their singing in my head."

Then she danced away and left me stunned. Angels around me? Holding hands?

Singing, *Protect this girl, protect this girl*? A five-year-old, completely un-prompted, with a vision of sorts. She had never said anything like that before, nor since. It still doesn't fit inside the box of my doctrinal training, but I know it was God giving out His tender mercy that night.

The next day I sat through an almost unbearable chain of events. In every circumstance, I heard in my head, *Protect this girl, protect this girl.* Those words gave me comfort and peace. And God did exactly that. When it was all over, I had been completely, absolutely and divinely protected.

I realize that story is wild for some of you. It's still wild for me, and it makes me cry. I mean, it makes sense. I believe that's the kind of thing God does—you know, the angels and everything. But that He would do it for *me* . . . it leaves me in awe.

Do you desperately need to know of God's devotion? Do you long to sense His tender mercy? Then ask Him. Right now. Stop and pray and ask God to show you somehow His devotion and love toward you. Sometimes I tell God that He's going to have to be really obvious, because it's just me and I might miss it. So ask Him for obvious, and then come back and record how God answers.

_____

_____

_____

_____

God delights to show mercy. (see Micah 7:18)

Before we move on, what about God's displays of mercy to you in the past? Can you remember where God has provided for you or protected you in a surprising way?

_____

_____

_____

_____

What about in regard to world events, wars, and rumors of wars? Nuclear bombs and chemical weapons? Do you need to hear God speak His protection and mercy into your fears? Ask Him again. He does not tire of your requests for strength and provision.

_____

_____

_____

_____

WHEN THE FATHER HOLDS YOU IN HIS ARMS

You know, sometimes it just gets to be too much. When life seems to be caving in, and you know that you are in the Father's arms, did you know it's okay to just let Him take it for a while? It's okay to allow yourself emotional and physical rest. It's okay to wait for His provision and stop working out your own answer. I want you to hear the Lord say to you, "Rest here in My arms; let Me take this now."

Sometimes we have hidden in our homes, run away from relationships, or stopped interacting or participating in life until the storm has passed. I realize sometimes that seems to be required. We have to pull away to regain our senses. But more than anything, I meet women who truly need a refuge for soul rest and restoration. They have souls that need to be tended. They have wounds that need time to heal. They need to laugh and be distracted more often. Are you one of those women?

I'd like for you to make some plans, and I'd like for you to understand that rest for your soul has God's blessing. Remember, He's wild for you and desires your refreshment and refilling.

Okay—first, I'd like for you to plan a personal retreat. Don't blow me off before you even think about it. Figure this one out and mark the days on the calendar. Use some money or no money. Involve friends or go by yourself. Get away. I don't want to be pushy, but one night won't really do it: two is better, and three is getting there. I could tell you how, but it wouldn't fit your life, so be creative. Get serious about getting away for a few days for your soul. I am leaving room for you to brainstorm and make plans:

Yes, I am going away.

_____

_____

My target date:

_____

_____

Who will go with me:

_____

_____

Who will fill in while I'm away:

_____

_____

Where I would like to rest:

_____

_____

Possible obstacles and their solutions:

_____

_____

Three great reasons that I will be better for having indulged in a personal retreat:

1. _____

2. _____

3. _____

Second, look around at your relationships, especially those with your family, and decide who needs to see you look into their eyes. I don't know what this is, but as women, there is a certain amount of comfort and rest that comes from pouring ourselves into the lives of those we love. When I have only been "maintaining" my

family, I feel given out and scattered. When I have determined to give in a fresh and conscious way, then there is reviving. It's weird, but significant refreshment comes from turning away from the hurricane and giving out love.

For instance, at night I can spin like a top getting everyone to bed, organizing backpacks and ice-cream money for the next day, barking out bath-time regimen. At the end of all that commotion, everything is done and I am empty. On the nights when I stop and call the children to sit on my bed, shuffle the UNO cards and deal a few hands, look into their eyes and laugh over the Draw Four ambushes, then amazingly, I am filled. It was a conscious effort to stop doing and take a few moments to give myself to them. In giving there is abundant receiving.

Who needs a little more of you right now?

_____

_____

What could you give?

_____

_____

How do you think God will fill you as you decide to give?

_____

_____

Third, could you laugh a little more? Please? Most of our lives are no laughing matter. Hurricanes are serious and devastating. But would you find someone who makes you laugh and stand around that person? I have decided that people laugh because they have given themselves permission to enjoy humor. It's okay, and, wow, is it good for your soul to enjoy a silly joke or funny story.

Do you remember the last time you laughed until you cried? How long has it been? Give yourself permission to enjoy and laugh again. Watch what happens in your heart and watch how people are drawn into your delight.

Now, lastly, in what other ways is God directing you to care for your soul in this season of life?

_____

_____

MY DELIVERER

The only hope we have is the only hope we've ever had.

When I was listening to a radio talk show one afternoon, a man, whose name I don't know, was talking about the impending nuclear war, the effects of biological warfare, the depravity of evildoers who desire to bring death and destruction to people all over the world. I kept listening, even though everything in me wanted to turn it off. The whole discussion made me have that deep sinking feeling in the pit of my stomach.

At the end of the show, the host asked his guest, "As believers, what can we do? This is all rather scary." I agreed and waited for an answer. The guest replied, "The only hope we have is the only hope we've ever had. We've never had another option apart from God, and nothing is different now. He is our Hope. He has provided our Savior." Immediately, my soul found its rest. How quickly I had forgotten: I belong to God.

No matter what your circumstances today, do you remember that you belong to God Almighty?

Do you realize that He is your invincible Warrior? Your fearless Protector? Your merciful Father? Do you know that He will fight for you? He is not afraid of anything or anybody. He is the One who speaks and storms become still. Is your hope all gone? Have you forgotten that God is the only hope you've ever had anyway?

When the Israelites were up against the Red Sea with the Egyptians at their backs, they decided they'd rather go back to bondage, because they could not see what God was going to do. Have you ever wanted to just go back to your old life or your old patterns of bondage just because you couldn't figure things out on your own? What did you do with those fears and desires?

_____

_____

Are you in the dark right now, waiting for a storm to pass, wondering where in the world God is? Claim Him as your Deliverer. Find renewed strength in knowing that He comes to the rescue. Trust that He will show up in glory to fight for you. Journal your heart's desire and your prayers.

_____

_____

_____

_____

_____

_____

BE STILL AND WATCH

God wants you and me to be still and watch, because He wants us to see His great power. What happens when we see the power of God at work in our lives? We learn to trust Him more. We learn to lean in closer. We learn to wait in the dark patiently. We learn that our God is really who He claims to be. We learn that He is truly our only hope.

Do you trust God right now? With your circumstances? Your difficulty? Your grief? What are you trusting God for or with? Will you lean in and trust Him more? Do you feel the weight of your great burden being transferred onto His strong shoulders?

How can you more effectively live in the power of trust? What would that really look like in your life? Where could fretting be reduced? Where could worry be replaced?

_____

_____

_____

_____

_____

If you are strong one day and weak the next, do not give up. Claim again the truth of Scripture. God is your Deliverer. God is your only hope. God is coming in glory to calm the winds and make a way.

_____

_____

_____

_____

_____

_____

_____

_____

_____

_____

_____

_____

Chapter Nine

HIS PERFECT LOVE

*If there is a question attached to the soul of a woman, maybe it's "Do
you think I'm beautiful?" When God answers from the depth of His
great love, it makes some of us feel like the wallflower who is asked to
dance. But we can become distracted from His invitation because of
the other lovers, whispers of unbelief, noise and clutter, and because
we are sometimes the prodigal, sometimes the elder brother. To return
to the music and strong embrace of God requires a desperate and pursuing heart. And when a woman chooses to remain in His arms of
devotion, God gives the only hope we have and His perfect love.*

In these next three chapters I want us to begin looking at the woman who knows
that God calls her beautiful. What does she look like? What will she sound like?
What difference does it make to be dancing in His arms? What can you expect to
happen as you begin leaning into the truths of God's wild love for you?

Many of us are laden with fears. I am hoping in these next pages we can understand and apply the answer that removes fear . . . being fully formed in God's perfect love. A woman who knows that God calls her beautiful is moving away from a life
of fear and running toward the strength that comes from perfect love. She is no
longer weak-willed or namby-pamby with her emotions. She is being renewed in
purpose and in vision. She is waking up to life and trusting in the hope God has set
within her.

I am excited about this last part of our journey together. I am eagerly anticipating the work of God in your life. What if these thoughts really connect with your
spirit and you hear the voice of God gently speak, "This way . . . over here . . . I have
so much more for you"? First it could be little steps and then a freedom to run as
you have never known before. I can't wait to hear what God will do.

Reread my stories from this chapter in the book, and then we'll jump in together.

JUMPING

I love the story of the bungee guy who wears the T-shirt that reads, "Shut up and jump." It makes me laugh every time I tell it. It also calls me toward reflection. When I think about talking instead of jumping, I try to take a quick life inventory: Okay, where in my life am I all talk and no jump? Where am I dreaming but not pursuing? Why am I afraid? What steps need to be taken to counter a paralyzing fear?

Let's begin with some fun. Have you ever bungee jumped or parachuted from a plane? Describe or imagine how it must feel to be falling and then caught.

_____

_____

_____

_____

Does your life ever give you the same emotions? If so, how?

_____

_____

_____

_____

How do you react when life pulls one of those loop de loops just as you thought things were coasting? Do you react with trust or find yourself worried with fear?

_____

_____

_____

_____

Does anything in your life right now require you to jump into the realm of the unknown? What is it?

_____

_____

_____

Is there a place where you are sitting in the dark and waiting? Where is the place? Describe the dark and the waiting.

_____

_____

_____

Do you feel as if you have been thrown from a train and told to find your own way home? How or why?

_____

_____

_____

I am guessing that for these or a hundred other reasons, you could be wrestling with our archenemy called Fear.

Read the following. Which statement best reflects where Fear is abiding in your life right now?

There is no Fear in my home. He has been kicked out and banned from the property.

He is standing at the front door knocking.

I let Fear in the house, but we are only visiting in the foyer.

Fear has stayed for dinner.

I am tucked underneath my cozy blankets with Fear snuggled up right beside me.

If you knew God was calling you to free-fall headfirst into an adventure, the one He has planned for you, what would your resistance be?

_____

_____

_____

Do you second-guess His voice? How?

_____

_____

_____

_____

Do you wonder if you are truly tied on to God? What makes you wonder?

_____

_____

_____

_____

Do you still question why a God like Him would want to catch a woman like you? What makes you question?

_____

_____

_____

_____

If the only way to conquer fear is to jump anyway, then how do we get there?

_____

_____

_____

_____

GOD met me more than halfway,

he freed me from my anxious fears. (Psalm 34:4 THE MESSAGE)

First, you have to know if you are on the right platform. Are you where God wants you? Are you pursuing His heart of love for you? Have you been still enough to listen for His voice?

Second, recheck the security of your straps. Do others confirm your pursuits or give you warnings?

Are you convinced in your heart that you are tied on to the unrelenting love of God? Do you live your life like that? Do you live strong and assured of His presence or weak and doubting His role in your life?

I'm fighting back the tears as I read pages 160 and on about the fears, the weak-willed woman, etc. My heart is so broken. My precious husband of 10 years says he no longer loves me and wants out. You have been describing me in these pages.

I know God is in control, and I have come against the spirit of control that has been alive and well in my life. I so want to give it all to the Lord. I so want the restoration of my marriage. Pray for me.

— Shelley

Do you realize that even if you make a mistake, you still belong to God? He can reel you back in and redirect your path. If this applies to you in this moment and you are living in the wake of a huge mistake, take a few minutes to journal where you are, how you got there, and your desire to know that God still has you.

THE WEAK-WILLED WOMAN

Go ahead and find 2 Timothy 3 in your Bible. I want you to see these words with your own eyes. This section might be painful. If some of this applies to you, it's not going to feel great when it lands. So prepare your heart and mind to receive truth. Pray about laying aside any predisposition to ignore the promptings of the Holy Spirit. If you get your feelings hurt or begin to feel a twinge of anger, then stop and ask God what's going on in your heart. Make sure you find out what He's trying to say to you.

Read Paul's listing of forms of godlessness in verses 1–5. Before we push past these words, do a little soul-searching and ask yourself if there are any traces of these forms of godlessness in your life. Write your thoughts beside each one.

- Lovers of themselves

- Lovers of money

- Boastful

- Proud

- Abusive

- Disobedient to parents

- Ungrateful

- Unholy

- Without love

- Unforgiving

- Slanderous

- Without self-control

- Brutal

_____

_____

- Not lovers of the good

_____

_____

- Treacherous

_____

_____

- Rash

_____

_____

- Conceited

_____

_____

- Lovers of pleasure rather than lovers of God

_____

_____

- Having a form of godliness but denying its power

_____

_____

Now read verses 6 and 7.

If it's true that women can be weak-willed, then it is also true that I have weak-willed potential. I know what you're thinking. I hate this. Eugene Peterson translated this passage to say, "unstable and needy." I hate that too. But the truth is, women can be fairly easily given over to "unstable and needy."

I gave you my description of a weak-willed woman in the book, but I'm going to

hit the high spots again here. This time, I don't want you to think about your coworker or your mother-in-law. I'd like for you to consider the characteristics of the weak-willed woman in regard to your own life. Which of these applies to you? I'm tempted to try and candy-coat this to get you to swallow it on your own, but that's not fair to you. If there is some medicine in here that you need to take, hold your nose and gag it down. Remember, we're just trying to get healthy, and sometimes bad-tasting medicine will do that.

The weak-willed woman can be:

Consumed with her fears.

Self-absorbed.

Caring too much about appearances and what everyone else thinks.

An invisible, frightened church mouse.

A loud, brash, dominant amazon woman.

Empty of ambition and passion.

Controlling.

Deaf to the voice of God, never hearing Him call her beautiful.

Full of self-pity.

Defeated by depression.

Harboring a grudge.

Prone to gossip.

Indulging her obsessions.

Easily hurt or offended.

Spiritually knowledgeable, but essentially without discernment.

Attending church and Bible studies, but never seeming to change or grow.

Given to a critical spirit.

Honestly, not for me, but before God, have you seen anything of yourself here? If so, even if it is only something very small, or if it is volumes, begin a prayer of transparent confession to God.

I want you to keep in mind that these struggles of our flesh are not just little sins to be dealt with. This passage says that any form of godlessness is a foothold for our enemy to work his way into your life. He wants to get into your house, scare you to death, beat you down, and keep you afraid.

The reasoning is almost circular. We can become weak-willed because of our fears. And then fear can quickly feed our weak-willed potential. The result either way is a very fragile woman.

> Say to them that are of a fearful heart,
> Be strong, fear not: behold,
> your God will come . . .
> he will come and save you.
> (Isaiah 35:4 KJV)

What do you think that you're afraid of? Write and think about the following questions.

Are you afraid of change? Why?

_____

_____

Do you fear more heartache, pain, and suffering? If so, in what ways?

_____

_____

Are you afraid of loneliness? Why?

_____

_____

Do you fear failure? If so, in what ways?

_____

_____

I am 52 and a "weak-willed woman." I have carried fear around with me for years. It goes to work with me. It stands beside me when I talk to the children. It laughs at me when my husband isn't home on time and I want to get into the car and drive past her house. How I hate this knot in my stomach. Somehow I want to be in love with God and have my own girls see that love in me. I don't want to be weak-willed anymore.

—Shirley

What about disappointment? How does it make you afraid?

_____

_____

_____

_____

And rejection, do you live in fear of being rejected again? By whom?

_____

_____

_____

_____

IN THE SAME ROOM AS LOVE

Fear is our enemy. It is like a bully that keeps coming around to pester, provoke, and hurt. Living in the same room as fear will make us incredibly weak-willed women. The bully called Fear might always get the best of us except for one thing—we have a friend who is bigger than Fear. We have a Lover who comes to our rescue. We have not been left alone in a back alley with a bully because we belong to God Almighty.

Yahoo! Now read 1 John 4:16–18. Underline the words that speak directly to your heart.

Here is the good news. The same God who has asked us to dance. The One who calls us beautiful. That God is called Perfect Love. And where we are fully formed in the perfect love of God, there will be no fear. Fear cannot be in the same room as Perfect Love. There is a way that overcomes weakness. There is One who does battle with the bully. There is a Rescuer ready to hear your cries of weakness and fear.

Do you hear the bully trying to heckle you even now? He may be saying things like:

> _Don't believe any of this mumbo jumbo._
> _This doesn't really apply to you._
> _God is not coming to your rescue._

When you are being heckled, will you learn to run into the presence of God and pray for His deliverance? How are you learning to get into the presence of God?

_____

_____

_____

Read again verse 18. John said fear has to do with punishment. We remain in our fears because we believe that we deserve punishment. What do you believe you should continue to be punished for?

_____

_____

> Therefore, there is now no condemnation
> for those who are in Christ Jesus. (ROMANS 8:1)

Do you know that in Jesus, there is no condemnation? Do you get this whole idea of position? Because of the blood of Jesus, because of His death on the cross, there has already been enough punishment. When we say that we believe that Jesus is the Son of God and understand that His death was enough to pay for our sins, then we have been covered. According to God, we have then been given the same position as Christ, the blessing of being called His daughter.

If you believe that you still deserve more punishment, then you are not fully leaning into this truth of Scripture. Put your weight into it and believe it. Jesus has already done enough. Accept it and rest. According to Galatians 5:1, God has set you free so that you can be free indeed. No more punishment necessary.

Do you realize what kind of woman you might be without your fears? Go ahead and try to envision yourself without fear. You would be amazing! Now that you have that picture in your head, what would you do, where would you go, and to whom would you reach out if you weren't afraid? Write it all down.

_____

_____

_____

Do you hear that tender voice of God calling to you? Could He be saying, *I have been dreaming of you without fear. Those aspirations are the ones I gave to you. I have you. You are tied on. Even if you make a mistake, I promise I'll catch you. You belong to Me. It's okay. Now shut up and jump.*

Chapter Ten

A BEAUTIFUL CROWN

If there is a question attached to the soul of a woman, maybe it's "Do you think I'm beautiful?" When God answers from the depth of His great love, it makes some of us feel like the wallflower who is asked to dance. But we can become distracted from His invitation because of the other lovers, whispers of unbelief, noise and clutter, and because we are sometimes the prodigal, sometimes the elder brother. To return to the music and strong embrace of God requires a desperate and pursuing heart. And when a woman chooses to remain in His arms of devotion, God gives the only hope we have,
His perfect love, and a beautiful crown.

We are still talking about what a woman looks like when she comes to believe God calls her beautiful. I just gave this message yesterday at a Beautiful Weekend, and if there is one honest comment that I still hear, it's this: "Angela, I hear you; I see God's answer in Scripture; I believe you believe it; it makes sense; but I am having such a hard time believing it for myself. I still can't believe that God sees all of me and calls me beautiful."

Okay, I understand, and I feel some of you nodding your heads in agreement. This is a spiritual battle. Satan knows what kind of woman you could become if you began to live out of the truths we've been discussing. He doesn't want you to ever believe God calls you beautiful. He is the accuser of believers, and he never gives up. The more you discover about the heart of God, the louder Satan shouts, "It's not so."

He knows all your weak places and presses into them. He can see your buttons flashing and pushes where it hurts. He doesn't want you to get this. He knows how much more passionate and purposeful your life will be in the arms of God. So keep this in mind: If something is keeping you from applying these truths, if you continue to stand back and question the depth of God's love, then maybe you have inclined your ear toward the accuser. Maybe he is playing with your head. And I'm sure he's pleased that you drag your heart around, making excuses, staying too busy or distracted.

The whole idea of our spiritual journey is that we would be changed into God's likeness. The accuser wants you to stay the same and even spiral downward toward emotional death. Will you decide to fight? Your life is too precious, and the potential too great. Decide that you will do whatever it takes—I mean it, whatever it takes—to walk in the truth of God's love. He really does call you beautiful. I want you to live like a woman who knows that it's true.

Read the chapter in the book again. I hope you have been looking around you through these weeks, taking note of women who seem to be dancing in the arms of God.

What is it about these dancing women? What do others find attractive about them? How do they inspire you?

WEEKENDS WITH WOMEN

Can you recall your favorite time away with women? Was it a retreat, mother/daughter outing, girls weekend away?

_____

_____

_____

What stands out as your most special memory from that time? Why?

_____

_____

_____

Have you ever had a time away that you would consider "life changing"?

_____

_____

_____

I just finished reading Beautiful. I have been on the verge of suicide, wanting to leave my church and my pain. The Lord used this message, among other things, to speak His love over me. I'm simply overwhelmed at how much He loves me. I'm still hurting but I know that He's with me.

—Grace

While we're thinking about it, as you look back through your life, what are some of the most significant "life-changing" events, decisions, or encounters you have known?

_____

_____

Have you been willing or hesitant to change through the years? Why so?

_____

_____

Do you feel that you have continued to improve in the past five years? Do you think you look more like Jesus than you used to?

_____

_____

Are you becoming more Christlike?

1. Are you letting go of old ways of acting?
   "Everything . . . connected with that old way of life has to go. It's rotten through and through. Get rid of it!" (Ephesians 4:22 THE MESSAGE)

2. Are you changing the way you think?
   "Let the Spirit change your way of thinking." (Ephesians 4:23 CEV)

3. Are you developing new "like Christ" habits?
   "Put on the new self, created to be like God in true righteousness and holiness." (Ephesians 4:24)

What would the people that you love say? Have they noticed? Are you brave enough to ask your husband, boyfriend, children, or parents if they have seen improvements in you in recent years?

If you and I had just been to a Beautiful Retreat, (and we kind of have these last chapters), and you were standing at a microphone to tell what God is doing in your heart and life, what would you say? How is God trading your ashes for beauty?

THE ASH HEAP

Heart-shattered lives ready for love don't for a moment escape God's notice.
(Psalm 51:17 The MESSAGE)

When a woman starts believing that God calls her beautiful, amazing things can happen. She really changes, and people begin to notice. In His arms she finds hope and strength and freedom.

Throughout this chapter I want you to think about being free from the sack of ashes that has come to you through the difficulties of life. Because you are dancing in the arms of God, you don't have to haul that thing around anymore. He wants to make a trade. He'd like to take away your ashes and see you wearing a crown of beauty.

Let's talk about the burned-out cinders of your pain. If you could look into your sack of ashes, what would be in there?

Have you decided that some things will just never heal? Some hurts will never go away? Some struggles will never end? You'll just have to carry them around forever? What are they?

Are you sitting in the ashes of a disappointing life? Poor choices? Guilt, pain, or suffering? Have you taught yourself to go numb through the years so that you can't feel the great weight of the ashes? Come to God in these pages and decide that you are going to untie the sack of your ashes and pour them out. When I finally began to feel again, everything had to get out. I called my prayer the outpouring. I ended up spending days writing the outpouring.

Can you begin to write or pray about the ashes inside of you that need to be poured out?

Maybe this doesn't make any sense to you. Maybe great pain or sorrow has never come to you. If that is the case, take some time to write a prayer of thanksgiving to God.

BINDING THE BROKENHEARTED

Sometimes we convince ourselves that because of our brokenness, we deserve the labels others give to us. Sometimes we get tired and decide this is just the way life is always going to be. I have a friend who was recently divorced and almost threw away her spiritual life after the process. Believing that she had miserably disappointed God, with those thoughts reinforced by close friends and family, she decided there was no use in trying anymore. She almost turned away from God because she believed He could never have anything to do with her again.

For a hundred other reasons, many of us can come to believe that we must be second or third choice in God's eyes because of our scars.

I love the passage in Micah 7:18:

You . . . delight to show mercy.

I don't think very many of us have heard or applied this truth. Yes, sin is wrong. Yes, we can make awful mistakes that disappoint God. Yes, there will always be consequences for willful disobedience. But still, God delights to show mercy. Do you remember the definition of mercy?

Mercy: not getting what I deserve.

Why does it take so long to cry out for mercy? I don't know. Maybe because we just keep telling ourselves that we don't deserve it. Ahhh, but that is the whole point of mercy, now isn't it?

Have you asked God for mercy in regard to your sack of ashes . . . your brokenness, your pain, and your sorrows? Spend some time with Him now and ask Him for the mercy that covers every disappointment and heals every wound.

_____

_____

_____

Now turn in your Bible to Isaiah 61:1–3.

Read these verses and underline as God speaks to you. These passages refer to the work of Jesus in our lives. Jesus even uses a part of this passage in Luke 4:18–19

_____
_____
_____
_____
_____
_____
_____
_____
_____
_____
_____
_____
_____
_____
_____
_____
_____
_____
_____

I do not feel beautiful, and have been treated as if I did not matter by my first and now second husband. How do I heal and begin to live again? I can tell other women how, but when it comes to me, I do not feel worthy. I feel unwanted and unloved and I wonder how God can love me. I know in my head that He does, but the hurt in my heart is so deep that it's difficult to understand being loved like that.

—Whitney

in reference to Himself. He is the anointed One who has come to preach good news to the poor. He is the One who fulfills the promises of this passage.

Let's walk through these verses step by step and discover what mercy God has for you here.

> The Spirit of the Sovereign LORD is on me,
>   because the LORD has anointed me
>   to preach good news to the poor.
> He has sent me to bind up the brokenhearted.

In this very first verse we have a reference to the Trinity: God the Spirit, God the Sovereign Lord, and God, the Messiah (the One who has been anointed). So the Son, Jesus our Messiah, has been sent to reach us with the good news of God's grace and mercy. He has come to bind up the brokenhearted.

I don't know about you, but I find such great relief in those words. I love that I don't have to figure out how to heal my own broken heart. Jesus willingly and lovingly comes to do that. Do you have a broken heart that needs mending? How did these broken places come to you? Journal the journey. And pray. Ask God for His mercy that binds broken things.

> To proclaim freedom for the captives
>   and release from darkness for the prisoners,

Jesus is waiting with freedom where you have been held captive. Are there relationships that hold you captive? Habits that have become unhealthy and distracting? Obsessions? Addictions? Indulgence beyond reasonableness? Maybe you are held captive by your own thoughts. You assume that you don't deserve freedom. You relegate yourself to wallflower status. You are afraid that you'll fail at new freedom.

Again, journal any thoughts that are prompted by the Holy Spirit. Where are you being held captive? Ask Jesus for the mercy that gives freedom.

You can have my heart if you don't mind broken things.

— Judy

Ask yourself if you are afraid of freedom. What would you do if you were no longer in bondage? Would you know how to rejoice over your release?

_____

_____

_____

Release from darkness. Jesus uses the themes of light and darkness many times in the Gospels. To walk with Him and trust in His Word is to walk in the light. To be apart from His fellowship is to remain in darkness.

Where is there still any darkness in your life? Where do you feel as though you can't see? Jesus wants to offer His light into your darkest place. Would you ask Him now?

> To proclaim the year of the LORD'S favor
>   and the day of vengeance of our God,
> To comfort all who mourn,

Did you know that our God truly wants to give you comfort where you mourn? He cares about every pain and suffering you have known. He aches with you in loss and grief. Maybe you need to sense the real comfort of God.

Sometimes when I am praying for comfort, I will lie on my face in my bedroom or even in my closet and wait. I wait until He really gives comfort. I wait for my heart to be stilled and my countenance to be changed by His presence. Maybe in your praying, you will need to wait quietly and even longer than you anticipated, until God shows up with the comfort you have been looking for.

> And provide for those who grieve in Zion—
>   to bestow on them a crown of beauty
>   instead of ashes,

Here we go . . . the crown of beauty. The mercy of God wants to come and take away the cinders of your pain. Understand that this is not a one-time life event. God promises to keep coming for your ashes until you stand with Him in heaven, where the crown of beauty is finally eternal. I love this passage, and I love that even though

I can be reluctant to ask, Jesus still replaces ashes with beauty. Ask Him. Remember, He delights in your asking and He delights in giving the mercy of beauty!

> The oil of gladness
> instead of mourning,

Yesterday my accountant asked where I go to church. I told him, and then he said, "The believers I meet who are the most glad go to that church." Wow. It's not because we don't have mourning, because we certainly do. It's not because we aren't flawed, because for one thing, I go to church there and I know my fallenness. I think, maybe it's because we keep asking God for His mercy.

Little by little, inch by inch, we are learning that believers are not required to live underneath ashes and mourning. There will certainly be seasons in all of our lives, but God comes and makes His holy exchange. Isn't it time to replace your mourning? Isn't it time you asked God for His gladness? Not the church-lady kind of gladness, mind you, but the real deal. The kind that comes from your soul.

> And a garment of praise
> instead of a spirit of despair,

My friend Nicole wrote an amazing sketch that she performed at Women of Faith conferences. It was about breast cancer, and it was called "Stepping into the Ring."[1] The whole idea of the drama is a woman's struggle with despair in the face of devastating news. The first time I watched Nicole's performance, I doubled over with sobs of grief and pain. It can be breast cancer that brings despair, but it can be a hundred other battles, like divorce, the loss of a child, bankruptcy, other diseases, and on and on. It's no wonder so many of us don't even know if we'll make it. The burdens are great. The load is heavy. And yet, for the believer, Jesus offers what we can't even conceive: a garment of praise. Praise comes to our hearts only as we allow Him to trade our despair for His hope.

Have you fallen into a spirit of despair? Do you need the hope of Jesus? He can give it. I honestly don't know of any other place to get it. But truly, the Son of God can give you and me a renewed hope that becomes a garment of praise.

What is your despair? Write about your despairing heart here and ask Jesus for renewed hope and praise.

_____

_____

_____

_____

> They will be called oaks of righteousness,
>   a planting of the LORD
>   for the display of his splendor.

Here we go. Here is the woman I desire to be. Here is the direction I feel God turning us toward. Do you see what has happened in these verses? A brokenhearted captive who has been sitting in the dark, with the pain of her ashes, mourning until she has fallen into despair can become a display of His splendor! How can that happen? It can happen because God delights to show mercy.

Think about that woman, the woman underneath the crown of beauty, the one who has been set free, the one who has traded despair for praise. Now think about yourself. What characteristics do you desire so that you might become an "oak of righteousness," a "display of His splendor"? Describe the woman you want to become. What would you look like if God literally applied each of these verses to your life? What would you do as that new woman? Have fun with this one. Dream the woman that God is dreaming in you.

_____

_____

_____

MORE THAN WE DESERVE

Redemption: When God takes something that seems to have no value or even seems to be a liability and exchanges it for something beautiful.

To receive a vase of flowers in exchange for a paper coupon seems like more than

I have been struck by the idea that women could be a whole lot kinder and understanding of each other. We could really encourage one another to pursue Jesus as the Lover of our Souls. After all, there is no competition for His love. He will dance with us all.

—Patricia

we deserve. To become a woman of righteousness and splendor after a lifetime of defeats, scars, and sin seems impossible and beyond anything we could ever deserve.

We have arrived at one of the most astounding characteristics of God. He always does more than we deserve. Our God is a redeeming God. He willingly takes a sack of ashes in exchange for a crown of beauty. It doesn't make sense. I don't get it. But I am so incredibly grateful for the truth of God's amazing love for us.

I know that you remember, but gifts that we don't deserve are called *grace*.

What beliefs, patterns, or choices do you need God to redeem?

_____

_____

Can you accept His willingness to exchange His good for your weakness as a gift of grace? Can you stop trying to deserve God and just receive His goodness and mercy? Go ahead and ask God to make the trade, His beauty for your ashes.

ALL OF ME

If the last few pages have begun to open up your soul, I want to encourage you to go ahead and show God everything. When a season of redeeming and mercy came for me, I knew that I wanted God to have all of me. I wanted to show Him every flaw, every sin, and every temptation I had been reluctant to deal with. I knew that He already knew, it's just that I had never wanted to own up to Him.

I had been great at skipping around my sin and woundedness in my prayer life. I'd rather pray for the missionaries in Siberia than fess up to my shortcomings and flaws. But then one day, while my soul was ripped open, I begged Him to go ahead and deal with everything He could find. I'm sure we're not done yet, but relinquishing my will was a huge spiritual leap for me.

The Old Testament psalmist cried these same prayers. Find Psalm 51 in your Bible and read the powerful words of verses 1–12 several times.

According to verse 1, where does God's mercy come from?

_____

_____

What about His capacity to blot out our transgressions?

_____

_____

It is God's unfailing love and His compassion that give us mercy when we cry out from our brokenness and ashes.

Now read verses 2–12 again. Do you hear the pray-er, pleading with God to cleanse away every sin that He can find? Why don't you take some time here to follow the prayer outline in Psalm 51 and ask God to get it all? Remember that He is huge in mercy and delights in giving it to you.

> Generous in love—God, give grace!
> Huge in mercy—wipe out my bad record.
> Scrub away my guilt,
> soak out my sins in your laundry.
> I know how bad I've been;
> my sins are staring me down.
>
> You're the One I've violated, and you've seen it all,
> seen the full extent of my evil.
> You have all the facts before you;
> whatever you decide about me is fair.
> I've been out of step with you for a long time,
> in the wrong since before I was born.
> What you're after is truth from the inside out.
> Enter me, then; conceive a new, true life.
> Soak me in your laundry and I'll come out clean,
> scrub me and I'll have a snow-white life.
> Tune me in to foot-tapping songs,
> set these once-broken bones to dancing.
> Don't look too close for blemishes,
> give me a clean bill of health.
> God, make a fresh start in me,

shape a Genesis week from the chaos of my life.

Don't throw me out with the trash,

or fail to breathe holiness in me.

Bring me back from gray exile,

put a fresh wind in my sails! (Psalm 51:1–12 MESSAGE)

Do you understand that you don't have to beat yourself up any longer? God gives fresh starts and gives them generously. He delights in wiping your slate clean. The next time you realize that you are in need of His mercy, do not hesitate, do not linger in your own punishment—run into the Father's presence praying Psalm 51! Come with your truth from the inside out and let Him set your broken bones to dancing!

THE CROWN

Do you know any women who wear crowns of beauty? Do you know a tender woman who has traded in her worthless ashes for a beautiful crown? Take a few minutes to list the attributes of that woman. What makes her so appealing? What draws you toward her?

Look at the list you've made and put a star beside the two attributes you'd like for God to cultivate in you.

I don't think you've missed it by now. God is truly pursuing you. He is wild for you and longs for your intimacy and affection. He wants you to dance the dance of your life in His arms. He has amazing gifts to give you, like this crown of beauty we've been talking about. What if you and I really began to live as though we believed everything He has said of us is true? What kind of women would we be? That's what we're going to talk about in the next chapter, and I can't wait. See you there.

Chapter Eleven

HIS BEAUTIFUL BRIDE

If there is a question attached to the soul of a woman, maybe it's "Do you think I'm beautiful?" When God answers from the depth of His great love, it makes some of us feel like the wallflower who is asked to dance. But we can become distracted from His invitation because of the other lovers, whispers of unbelief, noise and clutter, and because we are sometimes the prodigal, sometimes the elder brother. To return to the music and strong embrace of God requires a desperate and pursuing heart. And when a woman chooses to remain in His arms of devotion, God gives the only hope we have, His perfect love and a beautiful crown. God is enthralled by the beauty of a woman and calls her His beloved. He wildly pursues her heart with romance and intimacy to make her His beautiful bride.

It's never too late to become the person you always wanted to be.
— George Eliot

I am forty years old and for some things, it's probably too late. More and more, it's looking as if I will never sing and dance on Broadway. I don't think a letter is coming to invite me to compete in the Olympics. I could still go to law school, but I think I am deciding not to. And the astronaut dream? My heart holds it close, but sadly too much time has probably passed.

Thankfully, there is more that I have always wanted to be. I have always wanted to be courageous and brave. I have wanted to be hospitable and gentle. I have wanted my children to be glad I'm their mother. I desire to be captivating and intelligent. I want to be quick-witted and friendly. I value common sense and lack of pretense. I have wanted to be confident and spiritually secure. I want the clean heart that comes from quick confession. I want my life to matter for the kingdom of heaven. I want to know real grace and give it as freely as my Savior has. And I absolutely love that it's never too late to become the woman I have dreamed of being.

Because of Christ, you and I have our whole lives in front of us! Lives meant to be lived for His glory, with desires that He placed in our hearts. Longings that call us toward our purpose.

It's never too late to become the woman God has always wanted you to be. He wants you to be His beautiful bride. Don't hear me say that He wants you or me when we're perfect. That has been the point all along. God knows it's just us. A woman like you and a woman like me. Flawed. Insecure. Sometimes downright embarrassing. But not to God. He sees you and me covered by the sacrifice of Christ, and we are beautiful to Him.

Won't you reread this chapter in the book and come along with me for our final time together?

THE BEAUTY

How about you? What dreams have probably passed for you by now and what dreams still lie in front of you?

_____

_____

_____

If you have experienced a day of being the bride, remind yourself what it felt like from the inside out to be lovely and the center of everyone's attention. If being the bride hasn't come to you yet, then dream a little—what do you think that day will be like for you?

_____

_____

_____

Now here's the wild thing. Because you have chosen Jesus as your Savior, God calls you His bride. Those feelings. The unparalleled beauty and celebration. Being seen and known and desired on a day that comes to us maybe once in a lifetime. That is the experience of a bride. But there is so much more with God—He makes us His bride for now and for all eternity.

What amazing imagery God has chosen! A wedding is about the height of love, romance, and desire. And God says He loves you and me like that forever. Remember the groom and how he anticipates the beauty of his bride? God calls Himself the Bridegroom, and we are His beloved.

He wants us to know that He gives to us that kind of affection, attention, and love. The God of heaven desires you as His bride. He anticipates your beauty and delights in your presence. He comes as your lover, your defender, your provider, and your friend. He chose to call you His bride so that you could have a picture that accurately reflects the depth and grandeur of His love.

Now here is what I have prayed about for you during this entire book:

Will you live your life as if you are truly the beautiful bride of Christ?

Does this longing ring true with your soul? Are you excited about the idea or hesitant? Why or why not?

What obstacles continue to keep you from embracing this truth?

Then will you? Would you make a commitment right now?

I, _____, with all my heart and soul, commit that by God's help I will live the rest of my life assured that I am His beautiful bride.

Date: _____

I am 26 years old and already feel like I've wasted so much time not grasping or accepting who I am to my Father. I am being swept away by the truth and power of an intensely personal, intimate, loving God.

—Tammy

We've been saying it for chapters now, but can you imagine how your life will begin to change as you learn to live out of this truth? This is huge. This is where the wallflower hears the voice of God calling, steps out from the shadows, and begins to dance the dance of her life in the Father's arms. I am so incredibly excited! I don't meet many women who are dancing. I want you to dance!

THROUGH THE EYES OF A BRIDE

Let's look at the three characteristics of a bride that we talked about in this chapter. Except this time, I want you to try them on.

You are beautiful.

Don't squirm here. If you haven't gotten this by now, then we're going to have to go back and do this whole thing over. God has called you beautiful, and He'd love for you to begin acting as though it's so. The women who believe God on this one begin acting beautifully and thinking beautifully. They begin to radiate beauty and attract beauty.

How is God prompting you to act more beautifully in your life?

You are confident.

Maybe not just yet, but I promise, as you continue to dance in the arms of God, your confidence will increase. You will begin to act as if you know who is holding you.

Where do you lack confidence?

Maybe you need to stop looking over your shoulder. Maybe you need to stop second-guessing yourself. Maybe it's time to hold your head up. However you describe your lack of confidence, would you pray and ask God for the confidence that comes from a beautiful bride?

_____

_____

_____

_____

You possess unshakeable hope.

The bride isn't looking back, she is looking forward toward every new day with her groom. When your groom is the King of heaven, there is a lot to look forward to. There is hope. Persevering hope. Anticipating hope. Throw-a-party-and-dance-the-night-away kind of hope!

Proverbs says that a woman who knows who she belongs to can face tomorrow with a smile (31:25 THE MESSAGE). Is that how you face tomorrow? Are you hopeful about the days ahead? Do you anticipate the future with gladness?

How would you describe your hope for the future about now?

_____ **No trace of hope, obliterated, zeroed out, all washed up**

_____ **A random flicker of hope, but nothing of substance**

_____ **Marginal hope, hopeful that hope is coming**

_____ **Restful, get-a-good-night's-sleep, God-has-my-future-and-it-makes-me-smile kind of hope**

The Bible says,

that our hope comes from God (Psalm 62:5),
that we can put our hope in His words to us (Psalm 119:74, Romans 15:4),

that we can have hope because His love is unfailing (Psalm 147:11),

that our hope comes in the unseen, not what we can see (Romans 8:24),

that Jesus, our Savior, is the hope of glory (Colossians 1:27) and our blessed hope (Titus 2:13),

that hope comes from our salvation (1 Thessalonians 5:8),

that hope is an anchor (Hebrews 6:19), and

that hope in Jesus purifies us (1 John 3:3).

Take a little while to look up some of the passages above. Think about your hope for the future and where it really comes from. Do you place your hope in your retirement account, in the career that you've chosen, in the possessions that you own? Just where do you go to get the cup of your hope refilled?

_____

_____

_____

_____

If the Scriptures are true and our hope is refilled by the presence of God in our lives, His unfailing love and our salvation, then what are you not believing?

_____

_____

_____

_____

I want to smile at the tomorrows, but apart from hope, I will cower in fear. The bride of Christ is full of hope because she knows that the Bridegroom is wild about her. She knows that because of His love, they can face anything the future holds. The smile on her face as she walks toward Him comes from the hope she has placed in His love.

As God has been speaking to you in these chapters about His love for you, how is your hope being changed? I am praying for your soul to be renewed by the kind of love that a beautiful bride has for her Groom.

THE PRINCESS COMPLEX

I don't know where you are with me on this princess complex thing. Some of you may already have "princess" socks. We've already mentioned the "Sweet Potato Queens," women who are totally running with the idea, apart from Christ. Some women are really into the whole princess idea.

I have to admit it is incredibly appealing to me, but I have always denied myself from owning the desire to be cared for in such a special and lavish way.

Read again the words in Psalms that tell us how the King, the God who pursues us and tells us that we are beautiful, wants to treat the woman that He adores:

> Wedding gifts pour in from Tyre;
> rich guests shower you with presents.
> (Her wedding dress is dazzling,
> lined with gold by the weavers;
> All her dresses and robes
> are woven with gold.
> She is led to the king,
> followed by her virgin companions.
> A procession of joy and laughter!
> a grand entrance to the king's palace!)
> (45:12–15 THEMESSAGE)

Obviously, the King wants to treat the beautiful princess bride with extravagance. Now can you believe that's how God wants to treat you? Not just some woman back in Tyre, but you. He really and truly wants to shower you with the gifts of His riches.

How does that sound to you? Can you embrace this or do you still push it away?

_____

_____

_____

_____

Are you beginning to rest in His delight over you?

_____

_____

_____

I feel that there are really only two options: to believe or continue in the frailty of doubt. What if you get to heaven and find out that everything God said to you in the Bible was really true? Won't you wish you had lived in that truth? Why regret any longer the years we have wasted in disbelief?

I don't want you to miss the freedom and strength that come from believing so deeply that you have left no other options. As I review the next thoughts for you, I'd like for you to write beside each one how God is showing you it's true in your life.

You are beautiful.

_____

You are desired.

_____

You are held.

_____

You are protected.

_____

You are rescued.

_____

You are forgiven.

_____

You are pursued.

_____

You are seen.

_____

You are precious.

_____

You are His princess.

_____

You are His beautiful bride.

_____

THE DANCE

Well, my friend, we are almost through. Our time together is winding down, and it's time for you to make a decision. I think by now you have heard that God calls you beautiful. I believe you hear His voice calling you into His arms. I think you can just about hear the music, and you are finally willing to admit that those feet of yours can't wait to dance. So what will you do? Will you continue to stand around the edge of your life? Or will you get yourself on the dance floor and dance the dance of your life in His arms?

Spend some time in prayer on this one. Journal. Pray. Call someone. But don't miss responding to God on this. He is inviting you to dance. What will you say?

If you listen with your heart, what do you hear God saying to you?

_____

_____

THE WOMAN IN HIS ARMS

If you are the beautiful bride of Christ, and you are, then it's time to shine. It's time for you and me to begin acting like God, to whom we belong. It's time to let ourselves fully become the woman in His arms.

Enough of the weak-willed woman.

Enough of the distant country.

Enough standing around acting as though we are just one of the girls from the
kingdom.

Enough of the ashes.

Enough fear and lies and shame and guilt.

Enough of the church lady.

I want to be desperate for Jesus. I want to run to Him as He runs to me. I want
to want Him more than I want anything. I want to be changed from this shabby
woman into a likeness that bears His resemblance. I want to declare for now and for
all my days that my heart is fully His.

**Write your own declaration. Let them be your words, not mine. Make copies and put
this declaration of love and freedom in places you'll reread it often.**

Now, my friend, my fellow journey woman, my codancer, may I pray for you?

Oh, Sweet Jesus,

*Please take the heart of this tender woman and care for it deeply. Hold her
closer than she has ever known. Speak to her in ways that astound her. Remind
her of Your presence in light and in darkness. Comfort her with Your tender
mercy. God, please let her dance the dance of her life in Your arms! Let her
know the freedom that you have given to her from Your grace. Change her from
encounter to encounter into Your likeness. Let her finally believe that You call
her beautiful. Give her a confidence that she has never known apart from You.
And God, let her glimpse with her new eyes the hope You have set before her.*

In Your name and for Your renown, amen.

Now run with all you have into His arms. I can't wait to meet you and hear about
the dance.

ACKNOWLEDGMENTS

With a grateful heart, I thank Carla, Karen, Andrea, and Sue. Thanks for coming to my house all those days with your hearts for this project and your wisdom for other women. You are each great teachers, and I feel so very privileged to have sat at your feet, literally, taking notes like a wild woman, while you taught me about beautiful.

Thanks to Lisa Stridde, friend extraordinaire, volunteer assistant, amazing organizer, and beautiful woman of God. I am overwhelmed by your steadfast love and giving. Your whole family has been such an incredible blessing to us.

Thank you, Brian Hampton and Kyle Olund, for your editing and vision and enthusiasm. I continue with great thankfulness for the whole team at Nelson Books.

And then there is the best management on the planet. Thank you, Jim, David, J. T., Alicia, Amy, and Jeanie at Creative Trust.

Mostly, I am grateful to be held in the strong arms of Jesus. I am praying that my whole life is a sweet reflection of His glory and His grace. Oh, God, please use these pages to impact women eternally with the power of Your love.

NOTES

Chapter 2

1. Joy Jolissaint, *The Dance* (Tuksa, OK: Honor Books, 1999), 319.

2. Mike Bickle, "The Holy Passion of the Bride," *Charisma*, March 1999.

Chapter 3

1. Taken from Brian Irwin, *Connected Hearts* (Longwood, FL: Xulon Press, 2002), 292–93.

2. H. Norman Wright, *Always Daddy's Girl* (Ventura, CA: Regal Books, 1989), i.

3. Ibid., 193.

4. Ibid., 196–97.

Chapter 4

1. Mrs. Charles E. cowman, *Streams in the Desert* (Grand Rapids, MI: Zondervan, 1996). 65.

Chapter 5

1. Cowman, *Streams*, 70.

Chapter 8

1. elizabeth Ruth Skoglund with Charles Spurgeon, *Bright Days, Dark Nights* (Grand Rapids, MI: Baker, 2000), 161.

Chapter 10

1. For more information on this sketch by Nicole Johnson, visit www.FreshBrewedLife.com.

ABOUT THE AUTHOR

Angela Thomas is a best-selling author, speaker, and teacher who burst onto the publishing scene with her first book, now titled *Prayers for the Mother to Be,* which she wrote during her fourth pregnancy. The follow-up, *Prayers for New Mothers,* is a heartwarming collection of prayers written specifically for new moms. *Tender Mercy for a Mother's Soul* is a call for busy women to take time to care for their souls. Angela has a passion for encouraging women to nourish their relationships with Christ and does so through speaking engagements across the country. Women are drawn to her because of her honesty, humor, conversational style, and storytelling ability. Angela received her Master's degree from Dallas Theological Seminary. She lives in Knoxville, Tennessee, with her four children.

www.AngelaThomas.com

For more information on having
Angela speak to your group, please contact:

Creative Trust
(615) 297-5010
info@creativetrust.com

PRAYERS FOR THE MOTHER TO BE

This elegant gift book offers heartwarming, Scripture-based prayers—penned by Angela, a mother of four—that address the practical, everyday issues expectant mothers face. Simple, reassuring words encourage readers to have faith in God and bring all their awakened emotions and experiences to Him. The beautiful interior is inviting and uplifting. This is a gift that any expectant mother will cherish. [ISBN 0-7852-6386-1]

TENDER MERCY FOR A MOTHER'S SOUL

Sometimes moms get so caught up in caring for their families that they forget to care for their own souls. That's why they need the encouragement and direction they'll find in Angela's *Tender Mercy for a Mother's Soul*. Filled with solid teaching, heartwarming illustrations, and practical ideas for growing in a daily personal walk with Jesus, this captivating hardcover book will connect with moms in a very personal way. It will motivate even the busiest mom to take the time to nurture her soul. [ISBN 1-56179-904-1]

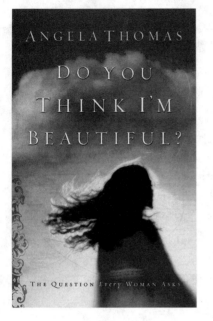

DO YOU THINK I'M BEAUTIFUL?

This book from Angela is for women who know, perhaps only deep in their heart, that they need an answer to the question, "Do you think I'm beautiful?" Readers will come to understand that the question is uniquely feminine, placed there by the Creator to woo them to Himself. Used, along with this workbook, women will learn about the distractions that can keep them from the One who calls them beautiful, what it takes to return to His embrace, and what delights await them there. [0-7852-6355-1]

Coming May 2004 . . .

A BEAUTIFUL OFFERING: THE LIFE GOD WANTS FOR YOU

For many years Angela thought of the Beatitudes as a list of "Gotta Be's," as in: *Gotta be* meek. *Gotta be* merciful. And when she compared her life to the standard they set, she always felt that she came up short. But through God's great mercy, she has come to see this passage instead as a roster of "When You Are's." *When you are* meek, there is a spiritual inheritance. *When you are* merciful, you will be shown mercy.

This shift in thinking has led Angela to understand that God does not require perfection, but rather our gracious obedience. In His eyes, our lives—complete with mistakes, blemishes, and imperfections—are *A Beautiful Offering*. [Available May 2004; ISBN 0-7852-6357-8]